RENEWALS 458-4574

DATE DUE

MAY 08			
GAYLORD			PRINTED IN U.S.A.

Practice Made Perfect
The Discipline of Business Management for Financial Advisers

by Mark C. Tibergien and Rebecca Pomering

"We hired Mark in 2000 to take us through a planning process for Accredited Investors, Inc. Since that time, our assets under management have quintupled, our infrastructure and management systems have been refined, our priorities have been modified, and we are working with bigger and happier clients. We paid thousands of dollars for his work and received a benefit far beyond that. Now Mark and Rebecca have put many of their ideas into this book. It's a gift to the planning profession."

ROSS LEVIN, CFP
President, Accredited Investors, Inc.
Author, *The Wealth Management Index*

"*Practice Made Perfect* is the ideal opportunity to spend quality time with the best financial-advisory business consultants in the country. You get tips, tools, and worksheets to ensure that you can manage your practice to become the business success you want it to be. This book will be your new best friend—guaranteed."

DEENA B. KATZ, CFP
President, Evensky, Brown & Katz
Author, *Deena Katz on Practice Management* and
Deena Katz's Tools and Templates for Your Practice

"*Practice Made Perfect* is outstanding. Mark Tibergien and Rebecca Pomering have captured the key strategic planning issues for financial advisers who are serious about making money with their practices. The ideas offered in this book are worth many times the cover price."

JOHN J. BOWEN JR.
Founder and CEO, CEG Worldwide, LLC

"Mark Tibergien and Rebecca Pomering have served up a real treat in *Practice Made Perfect*. I've known them both for quite a while, as consultants to our firm and as two of the most respected commentators on our profession's business management. I thought I had heard it all. Not so. Mark and Rebecca bring many new and important insights. Everybody in this business needs to read this book."

TIM KOCHIS, JD, MBA, CFP
CEO, Kochis Fitz Wealth Management
Author, *Managing Concentrated Stock Wealth*

"Most financial planners, including myself, start a practice because we love the work. It doesn't take long to recognize that if we want to be successful long-term, we have to build a business. Building a business is what *Practice Made Perfect* is all about. This book is not a how-to for starting a practice. Rather, it is a guide for taking your practice from where it is today to where you want it to be tomorrow. A must-read for practitioners who are serious about our profession."

ELAINE E. BEDEL, CFP
President, Bedel Financial Consulting, Inc.

"Mark and Rebecca are a dynamic duo—they are bright, insightful, and are able to get right at the heart of what is important in managing and growing a financial-advisory business. *Practice Made Perfect* is full of practical advice and ideas, which every serious financial adviser should know when managing their business. Their continued advice and this book are priceless."

GREG SULLIVAN, CPA, CFP
President, Sullivan, Bruyette, Speros & Blayney, Inc.

Practice Made Perfect

Practice Made Perfect

The Discipline of Business Management for Financial Advisers

By

MARK C. TIBERGIEN AND REBECCA POMERING

BLOOMBERG PRESS

PRINCETON

This publication contains the authors' opinions and is designed to provide accurate and authoritative information. It is sold with the understanding that the authors, publisher, and Bloomberg L.P. are not engaged in rendering legal, accounting, investment-planning, or other professional advice. The reader should seek the services of a qualified professional for such advice; the authors, publisher, and Bloomberg L.P. cannot be held responsible for any loss incurred as a result of specific investments or planning decisions made by the reader.

First edition published 2005
1 3 5 7 9 10 8 6 4 2

Library of Congress Cataloging-in-Publication Data

Tibergien, Mark C.
  Practice made perfect : the discipline of business management for financial advisers / by Mark C. Tibergien and Rebecca Pomering. -- 1st ed.
    p. cm.
  Includes index.
  ISBN 1-57660-172-2 (alk. paper)
  1. Financial planners. 2. Management. 3. Executive ability. I. Pomering, Rebecca. II. Title.

  HG179.5.T53 2005
  332.024′0068—dc22

                                                                        2004027809

Acquired by Jared Kieling
Edited by Mary Ann McGuigan

To Arlene Tibergien
and Grant Pomering,
for their indulgence

Contents

Preface

SO MANY OWNERS of financial-advisory practices complain that they don't have the time to do what they enjoy most—work with clients. If you've picked up this book, you're probably one of them. What keeps planners in such a vise? The answer is simple: the failure to manage a practice well. But how can you take control of your business? How can you help it grow, make it flourish? The answers lie in your approach to management and leadership. This book is designed to help you understand what strategic thinking feels like. It's not about pat answers; it's about acquiring the skills to solve problems.

Financial advisers often tell us their biggest practice-management challenges revolve around

♦ not making enough money for the effort
♦ not having enough time to manage and generate revenue
♦ not attracting enough of the right type of clients
♦ not being able to find and keep good people on staff
♦ not being able to manage growth effectively

These are the symptoms of a practice functioning in crisis. One of the great ironies of the advisory business is that many of its practitioners—even those who do an excellent job of planning for their clients—do not take the time to strategize, analyze, and plan for their own personal and business success. They get their strokes from dealing with clients, not from the tedium of practice management.

Effective management is a function of your ability to make decisions, your aptitude for evaluating data, and your commitment to your business model. Good managers have learned how to leverage their organizations so that the business sustains itself rather than depending solely on them. Our goal with this book is to vest leaders of financial-planning practices, investment-management firms, wealth-management firms, and other advisory firms with the techniques that make business managers most effective.

Acknowledgments

OUR WORK AS CONSULTANTS and accountants to the financial-services industry has been very fulfilling, so it is with great pleasure that we share our relevant practice-management experiences in this book. But there are many people behind the scenes who provided us with valuable content and coaching, compelling ideas and insights, and essential support.

We thank the members of the Moss Adams LLP Securities & Insurance Niche consulting team, especially Cathy Gibson, Ron Dohr, Philip Palaveev, Steve Clement, Stephanie Rodriguez, and Bethany Carlson, who eagerly challenged and refined our thinking throughout this process. Our thanks also go to Brenda Berger, Jennifer Long, and Lise Vadeboncoeur for keeping us organized and on schedule to meet our commitments.

We would also like to acknowledge the years of wisdom that Bob Bunting, the ex-chairman of Moss Adams, has shared with us to make us more effective management consultants. He has generously given his ideas and support to make us better practitioners, and we have incorporated many of his lessons into this book.

Our spouses, Arlene Tibergien and Grant Pomering, deserve a very special thank-you. The job of consulting with the financial-advisory profession takes us away from home more than is reasonable. When you love your work as much as we do, that's not a hardship. But the sacrifices Arlene and Grant have made have allowed us to pursue our passion, and they've done it with great support.

We also thank our consulting clients, as well as members of the Alpha Group and Zero Alpha Group, who have been willing to open up to us and who have continued to remind us that success in business is not purely a function of money and how you manage it but also the drive and desire to make a profound difference to the people you serve.

Finally, our thanks go to all the practice-management authors whose work has paved the way for ours and to all of the other consultants who have dedicated their careers to providing advisers with tools to be better at what they do. We're especially grateful to Julie Littlechild of Toronto's Advisor Impact, who has enlightened us with her expertise in helping advisers bridge the gap between serving clients well and serving them profitably. Throughout the book, we recognize certain individuals for contributions they've made to the profession, and we've attempted to weave in their perspectives as we addressed the issues we deemed critical to the book. Of course, no one book or any single author can provide all the solutions practitioners need, but we hope that what we offer here will help you knit together the fabric of a truly outstanding financial-advisory business.

MARK TIBERGIEN AND REBECCA POMERING

Introduction

WHETHER YOU OPERATE as a solo practitioner or own an ensemble firm, whether your business is commission based or fee only, whether you're a total wealth manager, a money manager, or an adviser who focuses on planning rather than implementation, this book will be relevant to your practice. The principles of sound management apply to financial-advisory firms of all stripes, and the tools provided here can work under any circumstances.

To understand the principles, consider how you would structure a management team if you could build your optimal model and you were not constrained by limited resources—whether they be time, money, management, or energy. Recognizing that your resources are finite, we will focus on the critical management disciplines you need to master regardless of the size or profile of your business.

Strategy: the framework for a firm, which informs all business decisions. As we discuss business strategy, we will walk you through the thought processes that can help you create a context for your management decisions. In our research and consultation with hundreds of financial-advisory firms throughout the United States, Canada, and Australia, we've learned that each business has a different set of parameters and perspectives to consider because each firm is unique. But whatever the structure, the work of sales and marketing, financial management, operations, human capital, and information technology is always better performed when the firm's strategy is understood. So at a minimum, practitioners must have a clear idea of what business they're in and how they define success. Management decisions become easier to make when you know what you want to achieve as a business.

Financial management: managing the bottom line. The information we present on financial management addresses critical issues such as benchmarking, budgeting, and management analysis. Financial advisers tend to give short shrift to the financial management of their practices, perhaps because they believe that simply having more clients will solve all their problems. The dynamics of a financial-advisory firm, however, require more active management and a solid understanding of what to monitor and act on to translate revenues into profits, cash flow, and transferable value.

Human capital: achieving effectiveness. In exploring human capital, we consider the concepts of recruiting, retaining, and rewarding staff at all levels. You can't be a true entrepreneur without leveraging off other people. Such leverage is part of the difference between managing a book of business and managing the business itself. The selection techniques, leadership concepts, and reward systems we offer here can help you reinforce your business strategy.

Sales and marketing: managing the top line. Volumes have already been written on sales and marketing, and there isn't much we can add to what has been published on this subject by such gurus as Nick Murray, Steve Moeller, Bill Bachrach, and John Bowen, but we'll tie in management concepts that allow you to apply their great ideas to your particular business.

Operations: managing risk, processes, and protocols. Within a financial-advisory firm, managing operations is often the most complex part of the practice; it's also one of the most important. Doing the job effectively hinges on how well you tie together the tools and processes that have already been introduced by industry vendors, broker-dealers, custodians, and other advisers. Again, considerable literature by such masters as Deena Katz, Bob Veres, Jeffrey Rattiner, Mary Rowland, and Katherine Vessenes is already available on varied topics as processes, protocols, client service, compliance, and outsourcing. Our review of the strategy, financial-management, and human-capital issues affecting your business will contribute to your understanding of business operations, but this insight should be merged with your own knowledge and with the information that's been provided by other experts in the field.

Information technology: processing information and communication. Like sales and marketing, information technology has been extensively explored in the trade literature, mostly because hardware and software have become instrumental in helping advisers manage client relationships effectively and make more appropriate decisions on planning and implementation. *Virtual-Office Tools for a High-Margin Practice* (Bloomberg Press, 2002) by David Drucker and Joel Bruckenstein is an excellent reference in this area, and Andy Gluck has written countless articles that can help you to apply technology more effectively in your practice. The big challenge is in knowing how to frame your technology choices, how to integrate new technology into your practice, and how to evaluate your return on this investment.

Our goal in discussing these management disciplines is to awaken your management skills and to give you a framework for committing to a strategy and for translating a vision into action. To accomplish that, we focus on the three critical disciplines of business management—human-capital management, strategic planning, and financial management. How you approach the management challenges related to operations, compliance, sales and marketing, and information technology will, of course, be influenced by the strategic decisions you make.

Some of the larger firms in the industry can afford to employ full-time management to attend to these critical aspects of running an advisory business, but for many advisory practices, that option is not financially viable. Owners who cannot afford a separate professional management team must master the essence of these disciplines themselves. But whether the work is done by experts or by the owners, the successful financial-advisory firms are the ones that have become effective in managing each of these disciplines. The management techniques at such firms are part art and part science, and leadership is even more challenging because it requires practice owners to create a vision and inspire others in the business to follow them into the fray.

The best way to break into that league of successful firms is to evaluate your business the way a physician evaluates someone who's sick:

♦ Examine the patient
♦ Diagnose the source of the pain

◆ Prescribe some solutions
◆ Recommend behavioral change for long-term health

That done, you're ready to proceed. Worksheet 1 in the appendix can serve as a valuable tool as you assess the condition of your firm in several key areas of practice management and determine where to begin the work of transforming the practice you have into the one you've always believed it could be.

Practice Made Perfect

The View from Here

I F RUNNING A BUSINESS were easy, everybody would be doing it. Managing a financial-advisory firm can be especially complex because the business depends so much on people and, over time, is at the mercy of events—from regulation to market swings—that can't be controlled. When these businesses start up, advisers are focused on their own survival and can battle most of these challenges. But as the financial-advisory business in general as well as the individual practices becomes more complex, advisers must anticipate and respond to a myriad of challenges, including:

♦ A slower rate of organic growth caused by competition and market returns
♦ Clients that are more demanding
♦ Difficulty in recruiting, retaining, and rewarding people
♦ An aversion to managing anything except their clients
♦ The pressure of margin squeeze
♦ The shrinkage of time

Slower Rate of Growth

The late 1990s created an illusion for a lot of people who invested in the markets, including financial advisers, who witnessed extraordinary rates of revenue growth tied to investable assets. This bonanza made many of them feel brilliant, especially those who had the wisdom to convert to a fee-based or fee-only model. However, the market correction at the turn of the century and the modest returns

projected for the foreseeable future have made revenue growth—
at least organic growth—more of a challenge.

Several conditions are conspiring against advisers who still hope
for rapid revenue growth:

1. Most experts predict long-term market rates of return of
   below 8 percent.
2. Inflation remains at very low rates (although that could
   change).
3. There is no longer an Internet bubble to give an artificial lift
   to the markets—and consequently to fees.
4. Many advisers have already reached their capacity in terms of
   the number of new clients they can add.
5. More pressure is likely on pricing, with new competition and
   more demanding clients.
6. If a firm's service offering is one-dimensional, justifying
   higher fees is hard.
7. Many advisers lack a well-developed, systematic process for
   marketing.

The good news, of course, is that challenge breeds opportunity.
There are things advisers can do, such as institutionalizing their
approach to business development and implementing a more rigid
client-acceptance process to maintain fee discipline. But it is impossible—and imprudent—to ignore the weight the marketplace can
exert on top-line performance and on the rate of organic growth.

Clients Demanding More

The illusion that dazzled many advisers in the late 1990s afflicted
their clients as well. Clients grew confident of double-digit returns
and early retirement; they thought they had become risk tolerant (in
fact, they were only *return* tolerant), and their feedback to their advisers was positive and glowing. As the markets corrected, though, and
returns dropped, many clients reacted with more needs, demands,
and requests, and they required significantly more handholding
and support from their advisers. For advisers charging fees based on
assets under management (AUM), fees declined at exactly the same

time that clients' demands, needs, and expectations increased. Some firms lost clients and felt the impact on their top line. Others kept the clients, but felt the impact on their bottom line because they needed to deliver more services for the same fee.

Difficulty in Recruiting and Retaining People

One of the most underdeveloped management muscles advisers have is the one for managing and developing staff. Some love the task, but most have neither the know-how nor the patience to do it well. Given a choice of where to spend their time, advisers will universally choose to be with clients rather than with staff. And since time is a finite resource in every practice, it's clear why staff development suffers.

The dilemma has a certain irony, considering that advisers are generally good "people" persons, meaning that they're generally empathetic, nurturing, encouraging, and fair in their judgment of clients—almost to a fault. Yet many of them struggle to employ these same qualities when dealing with their own staff. Part of the problem may lie in a perception that staff is a cost to be managed and controlled, rather than an asset that can generate a return. When the perception shifts from a cost-based view to an asset-based one, advisers begin treating their staff as one of their top clients, which has the potential to create substantial income and value for the practice.

Aversion to Management

In his excellent book *The E Myth: Why Most Businesses Don't Work and What to Do About It* (HarperCollins, 1985), Michael Gerber identified traits of the typical entrepreneur. Most were technicians, and many had worked for someone else before starting their own businesses. With the creation of their own enterprises, they were able to assert their independence, but they still viewed the business through the eyes of a technician. Financial advisers could be the poster children for *The E Myth*.

The joy of business ownership does not always come from building something but rather from owning something independent of any boss. For many, the desire is to keep all elements of a practice within arm's reach. So although their sandbox may be small, the point is it's *their* sandbox. Adding people, processes, protocols, and other disciplines to the management of this enterprise takes all the fun out of being independent.

The problem is that good advisers naturally attract more business. In fact, many have such a well-honed skill for developing clients that they can't help but grow. The dilemma is the more clients they add, the more staff they must add; the more staff they add, the more technology they must add; the more the business grows, the more their span of control expands beyond their reach. But does that stop them from growing?

Not really. There is a fundamental belief in the advisory world that "more clients solve all problems." Obviously, the inflow has to exceed the outflow, or your upkeep will be your downfall, but business success does not depend on income alone. If you fly at top speed, you run out of fuel that much sooner.

Successful advisers recognize that their business is their primary client: it's the generator of wealth and the cornerstone of their estate. Although the aversion to management may be natural, an attraction may grow if advisers look at it from that perspective. For advisory firms, success is defined by quality client service, ethical conduct, and the highest standard of unbiased, objective advice. Assuming these forces are in place, it's also important to define success from a business perspective—that is, as revenue growth, consistent profitability, a fair return or compensation for the owner, a healthy balance sheet, and value that's transferable. Without physical capacity, it's hard to sustain this definition of success.

That said, the solo model is a viable option for many, as long as they don't want to grow. The problem is most successful advisers can't help themselves. They do things to enhance their reputation, raise their visibility, and please their clients, which in turn results in more referrals. More referrals beget more business, which forces the adviser to add staff to serve them. Those who are committed to the solo solution should read David Drucker and Joel Bruckenstein's *Virtual-Office Tools for a High-Margin Practice* (Bloomberg Press, 2002) to learn how to manage the technology. But if staying solo or small is not an option, then advisers must work on improving their approach to the recruitment, retention, and development of staff and to the ongoing management of the business.

Margin Squeeze

During the market downturn, speculation was afoot that fees for asset management would be under severe pressure, with projected reductions of as much as 25 to 40 basis points. Some advisers have adjusted their fees because they lack the confidence to ask a fair price for the services they provide to their clients, but the reality is that few advisory firms have had to adjust their fees much. More typical of what's happening is that advisers are providing more services to clients for the same fees they charged several years ago. So although margins are not necessarily getting squeezed from the top as a result of fee pressure, they're typically getting squeezed from the bottom as a result of the increase in expenses required to generate the same level of fees.

Management of gross margin is probably the single most important discipline that an adviser can apply to his or her practice, as we'll discuss in chapter 8 on financial management. Not only is it important to manage costs; it's also important to know when pricing, productivity, and client mix are dragging down the enterprise.

Time Squeeze

Advisor Impact, a practice-management consulting firm in Toronto, did a study of the practice-management behaviors of financial advisers. In a question examining where the typical adviser spends his or her time, the results showed that only 39 percent of advisers' time is spent on client service. The rest of their time is spent on other tasks, like business processing and administration.

One reason time is so elusive for many advisers is that they're doing things they shouldn't be doing and have no one to whom to delegate work. Even those who put adequate staff in place may maintain a death grip on the processes and on the client relationships because they're not comfortable relinquishing control.

With his highly successful Strategic Coach process, Dan Sullivan has introduced many advisers to the concept of focusing on their unique abilities. But it's hard for anyone to give up what's comfortable and familiar and delegate appropriate work to others. Complicating time management, of course, is the general anxiety that small-business owners experience in not taking every piece of business that comes in the door. But one adviser can handle only a finite number of clients. Our studies show that advisers who call themselves wealth managers—meaning they deal with myriad complex issues beyond investment strategy and implementation—can handle no more than sixty to ninety active client relationships. But if only 39 percent of their time is available to spend on client management, how many clients can they handle effectively?

The combination of client selection, process improvement, and effective delegation will mitigate the time-squeeze problem, but having the courage to live by such discipline is another matter. Service businesses have only two things to sell: expertise and time. But when time is not properly managed, it's like watching your inventory walk out the door.

The Top Ten Challenges of Advisory Firms

To validate these assumptions about advisory firms, each year we ask advisers to tell us their top challenges as business owners. The top ten haven't changed for ten years, although the order in which they appear changes from year to year:

1. Lack of capacity to serve clients
2. Building value in the practice
3. Improving efficiency
4. Getting better clients
5. Managing growth
6. Offering value-added services
7. Keeping pace with technology
8. Developing specific expertise internally
9. Maintaining a life outside of the business
10. Time management

As consultants, whenever we observe a chronic problem, we try to find a permanent solution. But such solutions can work only when the owners of practices are willing to commit to changing their behavior. The problem is analogous to the problems advisers face working with certain clients. You calculate their retirement needs and evaluate their risk-management needs. In the simplest terms, the only two things they need to do are save enough money to invest and purchase insurance to mitigate their exposure. But what if they're committed to buying a new truck each year and to spending any excess cash on dinners out? At what point will they realize that the closer they are to retirement, the farther away they are from a solution? For an advisory firm, the same is true. The longer the practice takes to invest in processes, protocols, and people, the greater the likelihood that it will not flourish. So as an advisory firm begins thinking strategically about its future, it's helpful to understand where it is in its life cycle.

The Practice Life Cycle

Financial-advisory firms—like people—go through a life cycle. They are born, they grow, they mature, and they pass on. We jokingly refer to these stages of the life cycle as "wonder, blunder, thunder, and plunder" (see *Figure 1.1*). We borrowed this clever phrasing from Leon Danco, one of the leading visionaries on business-owner succession, who long ago wrote two outstanding books on the subject: *Inside the Family Business* (Center for Family Business, 1982) and *Beyond Survival: A Guide for Business Owners and Their Families* (Center for Family Business, 1975).

The challenge for advisers is to eventually align their personal life cycle with their business life cycle. Consider each stage:

Wonder. In this phase, practitioners are usually brimming with optimism, although some proceed with trepidation. Their practice-management style is seat-of-the-pants; they have no profits, no cash; and their clients look pretty much like they do. During this period, anyone who can fog a mirror is a prospect. If they're related, they become a client. The adviser focuses on volume of business just to survive.

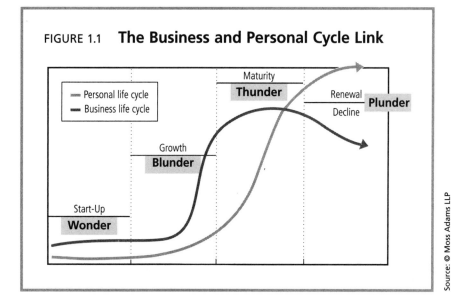

FIGURE 1.1   **The Business and Personal Cycle Link**

Source: © Moss Adams LLP

Blunder. In the blunder phase, business prospects are looking up. But this is a time of rapid growth, so the ability to manage is tested severely. Advisers in this phase come into the office early in the morning and leave late at night, continually operating in crisis mode, perpetually reacting to events around them. They're seeing an inflow of referrals and an increase in clients, but they lose the ability to pay much attention to either. Although income is increasing, cash flow is decreasing because they're continually reinvesting in the business with technology, office space, equipment, and, in many cases, people.

Thunder. This is the phase of the "harmonic convergence," when all the stars are aligned. Emotionally, advisers are more confident; managerially, they're more structured; financially, they're producing income for themselves at higher and higher levels, and their client base looks more like the optimal prospects they envisioned when they started.

Plunder. Although some advisers are fulfilled by the time they reach the plunder phase, our experience tells us that most practitioners are tired, burned out, bored, and indifferent. Some look to sell; others look to just maintain the status quo. For many, this is the time to harvest all that they've sown throughout their years in the practice. Revenue and profits will begin to decline as they slow down and as their clients die, retire, or begin withdrawing principal.

Where Are You in the Practice Life Cycle?

Some practitioners go from thunder to plunder in a short time, and some remain in the wonder phase for their entire career. It's helpful to recognize where you are in your life cycle, because it helps you to frame your priorities better.

In the first phase, the watchword is "survival." Everything you do in this phase is geared toward enhancing your personal reputation, building up your referral sources, and serving your clients well. Unfortunately, for most this is also the time when they know the least about the advice they're giving. And even more regrettably, the independent financial-advisory world does not have adequate internship opportunities for new people starting out, making the wonder phase a difficult one to sustain, finance, and emerge from.

In the second phase—the blunder phase—the watchwords are "managed growth." Oddly, most advisory firms experience stress fractures in this phase because they outrun their span of control and, in many cases, their financial ability to manage growth. Some will borrow heavily to purchase office furniture and equipment, fund leasehold improvements, or undertake marketing initiatives—or even buy other practices.

The watchword in the third phase—the thunder phase—is "complacency." Advisers at this point are typically brimming with confidence. But the seeds of destruction are sown in good times. During this interval, inefficient business practices—shaped by the survival and crisis management of the first two phases—take root as established office protocol. Client service can deteriorate. Staff development can be ignored. Often, advisers in this phase let their marketing muscle atrophy, because they have so many opportunities coming in from their referral sources. But as many realized after the millennium market bust, when assets started shrinking and clients started turning over, they did not have what it took to regenerate themselves.

In the final phase—the plunder phase—the watchwords are "renewal or decline." Usually, by the time a firm is in this stage, the conditions of shrinking client list, shrinking profitability, and diminishing client service have been in place for a long time. The staff at a firm in this phase begins looking around for new opportunities, and the clients begin asking, "What will happen to me if something happens to you?" The question for the owner is: Are you willing to reinvest the time, money, and energy to revitalize the practice?

We find the resolution of business practices in the plunder phase to be more of a moral question than a financial one. Most advisers develop a close, interdependent relationship with their clients. Because of this, many advisers are also reluctant to involve others with their clients. It's not uncommon to hear advisers say, "My clients will do business only with me; they do not want to talk to anyone else." For this reason, many advisers declare that they will "die with their boots on," meaning that they will continue serving their favorite clients until they're no longer able or no longer above ground. The moral question is: Is this fair to your clients? They've become dependent on you to guide them through their difficult financial decisions and sometimes even their personal and family decisions. But as they get older and more vulnerable and less able to address these issues, to whom will they turn if you die or become disabled?

For this reason more than any other, advisers should be thinking about their business model. There is a difference between a business and a book of business. A business is systematic, institutional, properly leveraged and staffed, and moving forward. A book of business is a client list, something that's harvested until it's depleted, a source of income, and a hobby farm. Those who are committed to staying alone and not preparing their clients for the inevitable—theirs and yours—are managing a lifestyle practice, not an enterprise.

So the challenge for those who prefer the lifestyle practice is to make sure that it will fulfill the needs of their clients even as it satisfies their own financial and emotional needs. Throughout the business life cycle, opportunities arise to create structure, processes, and protocols that can achieve both—but not without the endorsement of the owner.

Money is not the only thing advisers need to invest in their business. As we observe the evolution of this profession from practice to business, we also recognize the need to invest in certain skill sets beyond technical proficiency. Owners of advisory firms will be more effective in helping their clients if they can transform their enterprise into a client-centered organization that's not dysfunctionally dependent on its owner.

Defining the Direction

IN THE MOVIE *City Slickers,* the character played by Jack Palance asks Billy Crystal's character, "Do you know the secret to life?" Bewildered, Crystal's character says, "No. What?" Palance replies, "One thing, just one thing; you stick to that, and nothing else don't mean s**t."

"That's great," Crystal replies, "but what's the one thing?"

"That's what you've got to figure out," Palance says.

For advisers, that is your quest as well: What is that one thing that is the secret to the life of *your* business?

At the core of every decision you make in your business, every dollar you spend, every client you accept, every person you hire, is your strategic plan. It's the single most important tool you have in your business; indeed, developing a strategy and maintaining it are the most important responsibilities for anyone leading or managing a business. For most financial advisers, however, strategic planning is such an overwhelming process that it's frequently ignored. Many work harder to achieve their goals than they ever would have to if they had committed the time needed to plan.

What Is Strategic Planning?

The process of strategic planning for a practice is similar to the process of financial planning for an individual client. The same questions need answering: Where do you want to be at some point in the future? What is the best route, all things considered? What are the gaps and obstacles that prevent you from achieving your goals? What steps must you take to close those gaps? Ironically, though, even advisers who are adamant believers in helping clients plan for *their* futures often do not apply the same discipline to their own business, typically their largest investment.

Strategic planning is not just about marketing. Nor is it just about the process of defining vision and mission. These are soft concepts that many small-business owners have difficulty translating into action. Rather, a strategic business plan uses vision and mission as frameworks to identify the resources needed to achieve business and personal goals. A strategic plan gives you focus so that you do not waste your resources but allocate them where they can have the greatest impact.

Financial advisers usually preach diversification as the key to managing risk while building value in their clients' investments. For a small business, however, diversification is usually less effective. You have finite resources—time, money, management, and energy—to dedicate to building your business. If these resources are spread too thin, you dilute your ability to create momentum in the business.

Imagine if we came to you with $1,000 and asked you to invest the money in a diversified stock portfolio. How would you respond? You could not achieve enough breadth and depth with that amount, and you would likely tell us we did not have enough resources to diversify in a meaningful way. The same dilemma exists for most advisory practices. Considering your finite resources, how can you effectively spread yourself over so many strategic choices and still make an impact with your business?

Under those circumstances, is there any point in doing strategic planning? Ask yourself these questions: How old will I be five years from now? Where would I like my business to be by then? What will my role in it look like five years from now? What obstacles exist between the practice I have now and the one I hope to have then? Chances are high you'll see a substantial gap between the way things are and the way you want them to be. That tells you it's time to develop both a strategic plan and an operational plan. What's the difference between the two?

A strategic plan focuses on strategy—what differentiates your firm from others—and on vision—where you want your business to be. The operational plan focuses on the steps required to implement the strategy and achieve the vision. Many firms jump to implementation before they've defined their strategy and vision, and this leads to a lot of wasted motion. You don't hesitate to tell your financial-planning clients, "Investments out of context are accidents waiting to happen." The same principle applies to your business. Your time, money, management, and energy are finite resources. How will you concentrate them to create the greatest momentum in your business?

We recommend that you take a clean slate to identify all of the possibilities for your practice, without regard to whether you have the money, time, people, or management to achieve them. What makes this process so dynamic is that once you begin to dream—and design a plan to achieve that dream—you can also identify the resources you need and how you'll get them. For example, if you say, "I can never get to be a $10 million business because I don't have enough clients (or enough advisers)," you're confining yourself to conditions as they exist today. What if you say instead, "I want to be a $10 million firm in five years"? Now the question becomes a matter of what process you'll go through to get clients and staff to achieve this goal.

This kind of thinking gives you the context within which to answer the tactical build, buy, or merge questions related to how you're going to get from where you are to where you want to be. For some firms, the gap may lead to the decision to merge with or acquire another advisory firm in order to get access to the right staff, technology, market presence, or capacity. Mark Balasa and Armond Dinverno merged their Chicago-area firms with exactly this goal in mind. Independently, they each had excellent practices, with Dinverno's business being particularly strong in estate planning and Balasa's being strong in financial planning and investment management. Their merger not only added depth and breadth to their service offerings, it also gave them a critical mass that allowed each to focus on different elements of practice management and project an even bigger, more dynamic image in the market. Most important, their decision to merge was not based on economics alone but was rooted in their common strategic desire to be known in their market as a premier wealth-management firm.

The Strategic-Planning Process

Successful strategic planning is a comprehensive exercise. To be effective, it relies on a five-step process:

1. Develop your strategy and vision.
2. Define your client and service focus, including the client-service experience.
3. Evaluate the gaps and determine how to close them.
4. Execute your plan.
5. Monitor and measure results.

Steps two through five are updated annually; strategy and vision are reconfirmed periodically.

1. Develop Your Vision

The first step in developing your vision—that picture in your mind of where you see your business five or ten years from now—is to consider all your strategic choices. Imagine all the things you could possibly do with your business—the multitude of things you could be *known for* in your marketplace. Caryn Spain and Ron Wishnoff of Applied Business Solutions capture this concept well in their book *Strategic Insights: Decision-Making Tools for Business Leaders* (Oasis, 2000). They define "strategic choices" as the different ways to position a business for success. Applied to advisory firms, the priority you assign to strategic choices will define what your firm will be known for in your marketplace.

Using foundation research from the management-consulting group of Tregoe and Zimmerman, Spain and Wishnoff confirm that there are nine potential driving forces, or strategy differentiators, influencing the strategic positioning of every business. Under license with Applied Business Solutions, Moss Adams LLP applied these concepts to the financial-advisory business and found that the strategies of most advisory firms are driven by one or some combination of eight common differentiators. These strategy differentiators—and what the businesses that use them become known for—include:

STRATEGY DIFFERENTIATOR	FIRM BECOMES KNOWN FOR
1. Niche market firm	Serving a named market
2. Dominant local firm	Size and presence
3. Technical specialty firm	Specific technical expertise
4. Unique sales method	Unique way of attracting clients
5. Local presence of a brand	Major national consumer brand
6. Share of wallet	Cross selling of services and products
7. Standardized approach	Standardized process, high volume, low cost
8. Famous person/team	Identity of founder, individuals, or team

Although these strategy differentiators are not always mutually exclusive, each requires a different commitment of resources. And more important, the measurable outcome changes depending on which differentiator you choose to invest in. Let's take the "niche" and the "specialist" as examples. A niche practice is a firm that identifies a named market, then identifies and delivers the products and services relevant to that market. A specialist, on the other hand, offers a particular technical skill or product, then seeks out markets in which that service or product can be sold. Clearly, if you're a niche firm, you'll commit your resources to tracking the needs of your named market and then finding the right products and services to fulfill them. If you're a specialist, you'll be investing resources in maintaining the high level of expertise in a specialty, but primarily you'll be concentrating on finding and developing new markets for that specialty.

Christopher Street Securities in New York is a good example of a niche firm. It has created a culture that focuses on serving the gay and lesbian community. Everything the firm does is concentrated on its defined market—from the firm's name, which resonates in the New York gay and lesbian community, to the dedication to continuing education on issues such as asset protection and transfer, which are especially important to gays and lesbians.

An example of a firm with a technical specialty is Kochis Fitz in San Francisco, which built a substantial practice around its expertise in executive stock options. The firm's strategy has evolved and it has become a more comprehensive wealth-management firm, but this initial strategy was a unique way to differentiate the firm in a very competitive market and helped to launch it successfully.

We find most advisory firms to be generalists. They are generalists in terms of both their service offerings and their market, much as a local general practitioner might treat routine family ailments. When

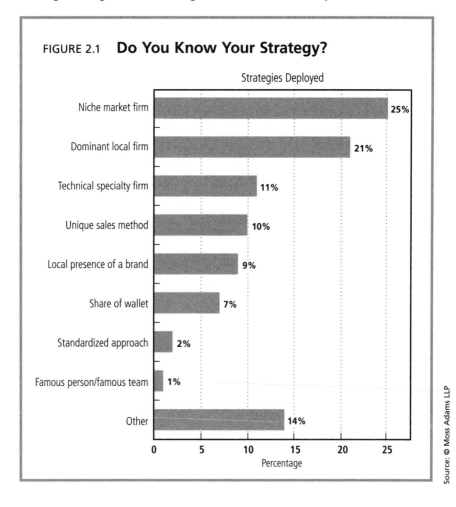

FIGURE 2.1 **Do You Know Your Strategy?**

Strategies Deployed

Source: © Moss Adams LLP

symptoms become more complex and beyond the doctor's expertise, it's time to bring in a specialist, such as a surgeon. In smaller communities, advisers become generalists mainly because there often is not enough opportunity to create market segmentation or specialize in a product or service area.

The challenge of being a generalist—especially when there is an opportunity to create a finer focus—is the risk of diluting your resources. Advisers are conditioned to think that diversification is good. They preach this concept to clients all the time, and they apply it in their investment allocation strategy. But why does one diversify? Diversification is a way to manage risk. It's a defensive strategy. Are you going to grow your business by deploying only a defensive approach? What will be your offensive strategy, the plan that propels the business forward?

Recent research into the financial-advisory community reveals the degree to which these strategy differentiators are being deployed (see *Figure 2.1*). These are the theoretical concepts on which you would base your real choices. For example, in a strategic-planning process we facilitated for an advisory firm client, the owners came up with more than forty possible strategic choices. As part of this process, we matched up the specific choices with the differentiators described above. Here are some examples:

STRATEGIC CHOICE	MATCHING DIFFERENTIATOR
Be known as the adviser to business owners in transition	Niche market firm
Be known as one of the top two advisory firms in the metro area	Dominant local firm
Be known for our specialty in executive stock options	Technical specialty firm
Build formal strategic alliances with CPA firms	Unique sales method
Capitalize on the nationally recognized brand name of our broker-dealer	Local presence of a brand

Expand our insurance, tax-planning, and trust capabilities with existing clients	Share of wallet
Be known for our effective use of index funds	Standardized approach
Build on the identity and reputation of our three owners	Famous person/famous team

Obviously, this practice identified key areas in which it could invest its time, money, management, and energy. But to apply these finite resources to all forty choices—or even all eight on this illustrative list—would be ineffective, and perhaps impossible. As an example, let's assume this firm decides on the niche strategy, wherein it focuses on being known as the leading adviser to business owners in transition. What are the implications for

- how to identify key hires for the firm to make?
- what type of technical training the staff would require?
- who the firm's alliance partners would be?
- where the firm would find these clients and prospects?
- which products and services to offer this market?
- what kind of administrative infrastructure the firm would require?
- what the most effective method of marketing would be?
- how many of these types of clients it could take on in a year?
- what its collateral material should say?
- how the firm would charge for its services?
- how it would deal with illiquid assets?
- how the firm will differentiate itself from the CPA, lawyer, and investment banker already in this market?

This is just a short list of issues that must be addressed when you pick a strategic differentiator. Each question begs more questions, and each answer requires a review of what resources you need to make the strategy succeed. Any diversion of resources away from this strategic choice into another choice would result in dilution. With dilution comes low return. With focus and commitment, your practice can gain traction and momentum toward its vision.

The risk, of course, is that you'll pick the wrong differentiator. That is why so many advisers hedge their strategic bets—again, the idea of diversification. But assuming you have evaluated your choices, looked at your existing client base, considered the competitors in that area, and conceived of a message that will resonate with the market, your probabilities of success are higher than if you had no conscious strategic positioning. With a long-term vision and a strategy to differentiate your firm in the market, you can confidently commit—and recommit—the resources required to win new clients and prospects while you continue to harvest income from existing clients. Over time, you'll see a complete transformation of your practice.

Any of these eight differentiators could drive your positioning. For each differentiator, an advisory firm may have multiple strategic choices. It's possible to begin with a list of thirty to forty choices for which way to take the business, and it's critical that you winnow this list to the vital few so that you can make an informed decision about which direction is the right one.

Most advisers begin unconsciously with a strategy based on personal reputation, or the "famous person" choice. When individuals do direct mailings, conduct seminars, get a radio program, write articles, or commit to clients that they will personally be managing the relationship, their personal reputation becomes their strategic differentiator. Their strategic choices are the use of direct mail, seminars, radio programs, published articles, or personalized service. Eventually advisers realize the limitations of this approach, particularly the inability to grow without becoming overwhelmed. The most logical progression for most of these practices is into either a niche or a specialty approach. If you look at your current client list, could you build either a niche business or a specialty business from the foundation you have? Do you have a group of clients who either draw on a specific expertise or might represent a named market?

Try the niche, or named-market differentiator, for starters: you may have a large concentration of clients who are business owners in transition, professionals, gays and lesbians, corporate executives, divorcées, born-again Christians, or individuals who've inherited wealth. Is there a common thread that runs through the group?

What specific needs have they asked you to address: long-term care, liquidating consolidated positions, stock-option planning, or inter-generational transfers of wealth?

If you can combine a niche with a specialty as a unique proposition, for example, you then can build your marketing and client-service efforts around these concepts. With a concentration of effort, you could then pursue a strategy to become dominant in that segment of the market. Sources of referral would begin to recognize you as a specialist in that market and, as a result, put you at the top of the list when the need for expertise in your niche or specialty arises.

Advisers tend to avoid becoming so narrowly focused because they fear they will miss other opportunities. This may be true, but it's a little like waiting at home on a Saturday night for somebody to ask you out on a date. Why not make the call yourself? At least you'll have an answer.

Caryn Spain introduced us to the critical concept of perspective. Perspective in this context refers to the points of view you should evaluate before deciding on your strategic positioning. For most advisory firms, there are four critical perspectives:

♦ Your marketplace
♦ Your competition
♦ Your current capabilities
♦ Your personal definition of success

Whether or not you go through a formal strategic-planning process, it's important that you continually revisit these points of view so you do not overlook important information as you position your business going forward. Here are some exercises to consider:

Your marketplace. Write down the names of your top twenty to thirty clients—not just the most profitable ones but also those you enjoy most and who also happen to be among your top revenue generators. Then list the characteristics of these clients, such as age, occupation or preoccupation, geography, net worth and income, special interests and special issues, and how they became your client. See if you can identify a common thread in this client base. Your goal is to discover what you need to focus on to replicate this client base many times over.

In addition to trying to find the common thread, you also want to forecast the issues that might affect these types of clients going forward. An effective means of doing this is to deploy the client-audit process described in chapter 3. What might the results tell you about the products and services you should be developing and offering to serve their needs? This exercise will become an important step in positioning your firm in the clients' eyes.

Your competition. Write down the names of five to ten of your top competitors. You may be inclined to say, "I don't have any competition," but that is obviously an illusion. Face it: if you did not have competition, you would have all the clients in your target market. So by identifying the top firms serving clients in your market, you begin your competitive market research. Go to their websites; clip their ads; ask their clients and your prospects about them. Your objective is to discover what differentiates them and makes them strong, what compelling strengths do they offer as an advisory firm? What are they known for? Then ask yourself: can we do what they do—only better? Or should we try to find a way to differentiate from them?

Your core capabilities. The mantra at industry conferences used to be that advisers should build their businesses around their core competencies. Although this is an important perspective, it's not the only one. By assessing your strengths and weaknesses, you can identify the gaps in your practice-management and service offerings. Ask yourself the difficult questions about your depth, expertise, responsiveness, talent, and even your motivation and interests. You'll discover the capabilities you can build on as a firm and the possible strategies you might deploy to shore up your weaknesses. It's an important perspective to consider.

Your personal definition of success. This exercise is an absolute must. Most of the well-regarded gurus on practice management— Dan Sullivan of Strategic Coach, and Bill Bachrach, for instance— preach this concept. What is personally fulfilling to you? More time? More money? Greater personal development? Owning and operating a larger business? The ability to spend more time away from the business? When you begin to explore this issue, you may also discover that you're not practicing in a way that fulfills your personal definition of success. You must ask, "What strategic choices would I make to achieve personal fulfillment?"

If you're part of a larger organization such as a bank, CPA firm, insurance company, or even a larger advisory firm, you may have to answer this question about personal definition of success from a larger, firmwide perspective. What would the parent company define as success, and how would this influence your strategy? Nixon Peabody Financial Advisors (NPFA), for example, is a wholly owned subsidiary of the law firm of Nixon Peabody in Boston. This business model has many interesting nuances because Boston law firms have the unique advantage of being able to offer trust services and manage money under a special state charter that does not require them to be registered. The creation of a registered investment-advisory firm is a form of brand extension that allows the law firm to expand its offering into wealth management and provide investment and planning advice to nontrust clients both within Massachusetts and in the other markets that this large law firm serves. One management challenge for NPFA is to be sure that its business strategy takes into account the expectations of its owners, the partners in the law firm. Those considerations include profit goals, reciprocal business opportunities, and not putting the lawyers' relationships with clients at risk. Beyond this, the lawyers must have clear parameters in their interaction with the trust side of the firm. NPFA must balance this perspective with its own desire to grow and expand business with the law firm's clients.

Sand Hill Advisors, a wealth-management firm in Palo Alto that's owned by Boston Private, is another example of a firm that had to adjust to new parameters. When it was independent, its leaders could make decisions about investments in the business, client selection, expansion into markets, and what it regarded as acceptable returns to the shareholders. Now the firm must be responsive to the owners who acquired it. Although some may chafe under such expectations, in reality, these parameters give Sand Hill a discipline in management it may not have had while it was independently owned. Furthermore, having a successful parent also gives firms like Sand Hill greater access to resources to better serve their clients, and that's the potential payback.

Tying it together. As you examine your strategic choices from these four perspectives, your priorities begin to take shape. Eventually, you'll land on a primary strategy that's supported by the others, and it will serve as your framework for making future business decisions. It will also help you to take some things off the table that have been a distraction, like the addition of new business lines, the addition of staff members who do not really serve your core clients, or even the acceptance of certain clients.

Your strategy for your business, then, will be one that
♦ responds to your market
♦ differentiates you from your competition
♦ builds on your core capabilities
♦ fulfills your personal definition of success

A one-dimensional strategy will likely lead you in the wrong direction. But an approach that considers your choices from these four critical perspectives will allow you to have a four-dimensional view of what your business needs to look like in the future. And when you can answer the question "What do I want my business to look like in the future?" you have a vision.

By using a structured strategic-planning process, called the Practice Navigator™, with advisers we discovered that many financial advisers have made strategic choices in their practices that could differentiate them. Many of the same advisers, however, have not gotten past the thinking stage into the action stage. As a result, they have not transformed strategic choices into measurable results. To achieve meaningful results, it's essential to commit to a primary strategic differentiator. Commitment means your culture, your processes, your product and service offerings, your people, and your financial performance all align with how you're strategically positioning, or differentiating, your firm in the marketplace. For example, Ross Levin and Will Heupel of Accredited Investors in Edina, Minnesota, recognized they wanted their practice to be perceived as a high-value financial-planning and advisory firm serving individuals who have complex planning issues and could justify paying fees in excess of $10,000 a year. This decision allowed Accredited Investors to broaden its client base to include those who have investable assets exceeding $1 million and have genuine planning issues. But the desire to serve wealthier clients is not in itself a sufficient differentiator. So in their strategic positioning, they deploy the Wealth Management Index™, a proprietary process developed by Levin to help the firm take a more comprehensive approach to implementing, measuring, and monitoring a client's plan. This approach keeps clients from judging the firm solely on investment performance and underscores the value it delivers beyond investment selection.

To make this approach work, the firm needed to define the client-service experience, which included how it was going to report to the clients. The owners also had to make the internal commitment to applying this process to all of their clients to ensure consistency in their process and protocols. Individual jobs were redefined to support it. Technology was designed to enhance it. The marketing came naturally, as an outgrowth of a clearly defined process, and the firm has become known and differentiated itself in its marketplace for this specialty. This is a good example of strategic positioning.

2. Define Your Focus

The process of considering all the possibilities of what you could possibly do with your business is both exhilarating and exhausting. After determining the priorities that will define your business in the future, you need to further refine your vision by answering these important questions:

♦ Which clients will we serve and why?
♦ Which products and services will we offer and why?
♦ How do we deliver those products and services to those clients in a way that makes us unique?

Each of these questions requires an answer before you can proceed. Worksheet 2, "Analysis of Top Twenty Clients," in the appendix will give you a framework for evaluating those clients most appropriate to your defined business strategy—their common characteristics and needs—and allow you to begin thinking about where and how you might be able to replicate those core clients.

For example, if you decide that your target market is "business owners in transition," it's important that you both quantify and qualify this market:

♦ Where will you focus geographically?
♦ What size businesses will you target?
♦ On which industries will you focus?
♦ At what stage in their life cycle is it best to reach out to them?

Once you complete this process, it will become easier to predict the issues these prospective clients will be facing over the next three to five years and develop a product and service offering that's geared to this market. If you make a commitment to business owners in transition, for example, you'll need to be aware of issues related to:

♦ Family and money dynamics
♦ Retirement planning
♦ Management development and succession
♦ Estate planning
♦ Risk management
♦ Ownership transition options
♦ Business financing
♦ Merger and acquisition deal structures
♦ Marital and divorce entitlements
♦ Business planning and financial modeling

None of these issues has a direct relationship to investment management (which may be your primary income driver), but they greatly influence how you will prepare your clients for the transition. Will you personally become the expert in these areas, or will you need to merge, or structure alliances, or hire talent to fulfill the product and service offerings needed in this market? Once again, any choice of strategy results in another long list of questions, answers, and resource needs. To be the master of your domain, however, you must examine the implications of your strategic positioning beyond the sales and marketing. A sharper focus is key.

With a well-defined strategy and a finer focus on who your optimal client is, your challenge now is how to create the client-service experience that's geared specifically to this optimal client. To accomplish this, you need to break down the process into its essential components. For example, your client process may look something like this:

◆ Initial promotion
◆ Prospect responds
◆ First meeting
◆ Relationship defined
◆ Information gathered
◆ Analysis performed
◆ Recommendations developed
◆ Internal quality control review done on the recommendations
◆ Recommendations made to the client
◆ Recommendations implemented by the adviser
◆ Actions confirmed to the client
◆ Follow-up meetings held

Of course, this process has countless variations, depending entirely on your philosophy and approach. Over time, you find the way that works best for you. For example, if all of your new business comes from referrals, it's possible you would include a step about how you communicate with the sources of referral. Or you may have a more aggressive business-development initiative that requires multiple contacts with prospects before they become clients. Whatever your process is, isolate it, document what makes it successful, and train your staff in the protocol.

Beyond the process, there is also your philosophy of client service to consider. For example, if you require that all new clients have a financial plan, then what will be the components of that plan? Or if you insist that you be made aware of your client's total financial picture, including any investments with other advisers, then define how and why this is being done. Although these considerations may seem elementary, we find that many advisers approach their clients as if it's their very first experience at advice giving. There is no need to be tentative. If your logic is sound, your approach consistent, and your fees are reasonable for what you're delivering, then make it clear to your prospect or client how you do business. Can you imagine a doctor wanting to treat a patient who tells the physician what the approach should be? Or a CPA being comfortable auditing only those documents the business executive chooses to make available—Enron notwithstanding?

Of course, to most advisers who have run their own practices, this may seem like tortuous bureaucracy. As one adviser put it, "Look, I sell it [and] then move on to the next one. Why do I want to get bogged down in all these steps?" The most compelling reason is to institutionalize your practice and develop a means for leveraging your time. If you can't define the steps or what the client can expect, how can you hire or train anybody to help you do it well?

So with each step delineated, it becomes clearer how to assign accountability. And with roles defined, it's easier to design the right organization. Some of the functions are clerical, others are mid-level professional, and some are senior-level professional. We'll discuss the development of roles, responsibilities, and organizational models further in later sections.

3. Evaluate the Gaps

A strategy projects a vision of where you want to be, not where you are. The goal might be to sell the business, to provide a more stable income driver, or to leave a legacy. By definition, goals are long range; objectives are short range.

It's common in small businesses to think of the SWOT—strengths, weaknesses, opportunities, and threats—analysis as strategic planning, and too many planning processes begin and end there. The mistake with this approach is that when firms evaluate their SWOT, it's often done in the context of the current conditions of the business—where the business is—without the perspective of where they want the business to be. Done properly, and at the appropriate point in the comprehensive strategic-planning process, the SWOT analysis becomes a crucial part of the process, because it allows you to evaluate the barriers to achieving your goals and the strengths and opportunities on which to leverage.

When doing a SWOT analysis, ask these questions:

◆ What internal strengths can we build on to achieve our vision and reinforce our differentiation?

◆ What weaknesses exist inside the firm that could undermine our vision and differentiation?

♦ What external opportunities can we capitalize on to achieve our vision and leverage our differentiation?
♦ What external threats exist that could keep us from our goal and undermine our differentiation?

In this way, and at this point in the planning process, you assess your SWOT in light of where you're going, not just in light of where you are. When you examine these gaps in your strategic positioning, the efforts—or goals—requiring focus will become apparent. Not all goals are financial, although revenue and operating profitability are two goals we recommend be included in almost all strategic plans. Your goals should support your strategic positioning and may be related to efforts to enhance market position, reduce staff turnover, increase productivity, or expand referrals from specific sources. To see how you apply this concept to your business, let's look at the SWOT analysis done by an advisory firm we helped to develop a strategy.

SWOT analysis. The planning team evaluated the firm's internal strengths and weaknesses and external opportunities and threats in relation to the agreed-on vision.

Internal strengths
♦ Caring attitude toward clients
♦ Passion for business
♦ Experience of professional staff
♦ Investment process
♦ Documentation of client information
♦ Compliance history
♦ Comprehensive nature of advice

Internal weaknesses
♦ Organizational design
♦ Client satisfaction
♦ Practice management
♦ Time management
♦ Fear of growth
♦ Staff turnover

♦ Lacking tools to serve certain markets
♦ Internal communication
♦ Firm profitability
♦ Dependency on owner
♦ Morale
♦ Compensation alignment
♦ Capacity to grow the business
♦ Time-consuming processes (inefficiency)

External opportunities
♦ Domestic partners
♦ Aging baby boomers
♦ Inheritors
♦ Widows
♦ Business owner transition
♦ Increased demand by the public in general
♦ No dominant adviser in the market
♦ Communication with clients

External threats
♦ Market performance
♦ Competition
♦ Secular bear market
♦ Terrorism
♦ Changes in tax law
♦ Investor behavior
♦ Regulatory climate
♦ Media
♦ Scandals
♦ An attorney general
♦ Sensitivity to fees

Following the SWOT discussion, the planning team considered the question: What goals can we accomplish over the next five years to build on our strengths, shore up our weaknesses, capitalize on our opportunities, and protect against any threats? The team brainstormed a number of goals to achieve in the next five years, including:

1. Implement a compensation policy that aligns with business, team, and individual goals
2. Create an environment that allows people to grow and flourish
3. Develop and deliver financial plans efficiently and effectively
4. Increase the ratio of optimal clients
5. Increase the number of optimal-client referrals from clients
6. Minimize the labor element of planning and investment process
7. Maintain an operating profit of >25 percent, gross profit margin of >60 percent
8. Develop a team-based organization
9. Create a career path for staff
10. Improve staff-satisfaction evaluations
11. Improve compliance evaluation from broker-dealer
12. Improve client-satisfaction scores
13. Increase the number of domestic-partner clients
14. Increase the number of sudden-wealth clients
15. Maintain a consistent, predictable revenue stream

Though the temptation is to say, "Yes! We can get all of these things done in the next five years!" realistically most firms do not have the resources to commit in a meaningful way to more than five to seven goals. The planning team narrowed this list of fifteen prospective goals down to six achievable and desirable goals to reinforce the culture they wanted to develop, the clients they want to serve, and the financial performance they wish to attain:

Goal 1: Create a career path for staff
Goal 2: Improve client-satisfaction scores
Goal 3: Increase the ratio of optimal clients
Goal 4: Develop a team-based organization
Goal 5: Maintain a consistent, predictable revenue stream
Goal 6: Maintain an operating profit margin of >25 percent

Each of these goals helps to close the gaps identified in the SWOT analysis while aligning with the firm's strategic choices and differentiator, which consisted of

♦ differentiating by emphasizing team approach to being personal CFO
♦ being known for having a superior approach to comprehensive financial planning
♦ differentiating by offering a comprehensive review process
♦ being efficient at client-migration management
♦ responding to the needs of retirees

The challenge at this point is to develop an implementation plan that will move the firm incrementally closer to achieving its goals.

4. Execute Your Plan

When implementing a strategic plan, it's most important to make incremental progress. The temptation is to take giant steps when baby steps will do. If you're like most financial advisers, too many things are competing for your attention, not the least of which are your current clients. Incremental progress means taking on tasks that move you closer to the goal.

After you have narrowed down your long-term goals to a list of five to seven, consider what needs to be done over the next twelve months to move incrementally closer to each one. Identify the resources you'll require to complete those objectives, assign accountability, and establish a timeline.

It's best to put these tasks into a matrix to see if any one person is overwhelmed, or any one task will require more attention to be completed. For example, if all of the tasks on your list are scheduled for completion in the first quarter, and only one person is made accountable to complete these tasks, you're likely to fail. A task that doesn't make your list this first quarter or first year can be rolled over into the second quarter or year. Effective business management requires that you continually address the issues that require attention, but it also requires that you recognize that not every action carries equal weight.

Effective execution of a plan requires that you plan specific, measurable steps, a timeline, and accountability. As you develop the tasks to support the goals, make sure you're clear on the following:
♦ What outcome do we want?
♦ What action is required?

♦ Who is accountable to ensure it gets done?
♦ What impact do we expect this tactic will have on the business?
♦ How will we monitor and report on its success or completion?

When you identify which tasks you plan to address during the coming twelve months, express them in terms of these questions. For example, in the case outlined above, specific objectives for the first two goals might include:

GOAL 1	PROVIDE A CAREER PATH FOR STAFF
Action	Develop benchmarks for advancement at different levels
Due date	March 31
Accountability	Hillary
Impact	Helps staff and supervisor recognize progress in development
Monitoring/ reporting	Semiannual staff evaluations will demonstrate progress

GOAL 2	IMPROVE CLIENT-SATISFACTION SCORES
Action	Implement client survey to assess needs, interests, and satisfaction
Due date	April 30
Accountability	William
Impact	Institutionalizes feedback from clients to support personal interaction
Monitoring/ reporting	Monthly client report, which produces quantitative and qualitative information

In these two examples, specific tactics relate to specific goals. The first goal is to have a clearly defined career path for staff. This goal is interesting for several reasons, not the least of which is that it does not directly relate to producing more revenue. That may be a by-product, but in this case, the owners of the advisory firm were more interested in growing the firm's capacity, enhancing its team approach, and providing an environment attractive to top talent in the business. The supporting tactic is very specific—create benchmarks. The strategic-planning team recognized that it needed to develop targets to define career advancement. With a target, the firm will know what to coach to. But this is an important first step to take even before it begins recruiting new people, and it will help in evaluating how well people are advancing. The tactic has a short-term orientation (March 31); somebody accountable to get it done (Hillary); and a prescribed means of tracking progress (semiannual reviews).

The second goal in this example is related to client service. The strategic-planning team had been frustrated that the firm was spending less time on its most valued clients than it knew it should, and so it created a specific goal to address this issue.

Once you set out each of these tasks and tactics into a matrix and organize them by both timeline and accountability, you'll be able to observe whether they're too much to take on at this time. The point of incremental progress is to move forward. Overreaching is like overexercising—you wind up sore and paralyzed and eventually lose interest in the pursuit of your goal. Outlining realistic goals and individual accountability and moving the business incrementally closer to where you want it to be are key to successfully executing your plan.

5. Monitor and Measure Results

To track the progress of a plan, you must have both a means to measure success and a metric. The measure should be results oriented, not process oriented, meaning that there's a specific outcome expected. For example:

- ♦ An increase in revenue of $5 million
- ♦ An operating profit margin of 23 percent
- ♦ Attrition of A-list clients limited to 2 percent of the total
- ♦ Revenue per client of $10,000
- ♦ Revenue per professional staff member of $300,000

These measures serve as your mileposts. And each year, you should be tracking whether you're moving incrementally closer to the goal.

Each practice is unique; therefore, what's measured is unique to that practice. That said, every practice should attempt to evaluate certain broad areas of operating performance. We'll discuss these areas in more detail in the sections on financial management and human capital, but here are some key metrics for you to observe each year over a period of several years to observe a trend:

- Revenue per client
- Revenue per staff member
- Revenue per professional staff member
- Operating profit per client
- Operating profit per staff member
- Operating profit per professional staff member
- Active clients per staff member
- Active clients per professional staff member

Each of these measures is a leading indicator, especially when observed over time. From an operating perspective, they give you insight as to whether you're achieving your practice-management goals. In general, other areas to observe when measuring the effectiveness of your strategy should include:

- Client satisfaction
- Client turnover
- Staff turnover
- Turnaround time on the delivery of plans
- Execution of transactions
- Timeliness of reports
- Growth

Although the list of possible measures is endless, the key is to employ those that support your goals and tactics and to establish meaningful metrics that prompt you to reach for those goals but not to overextend.

Recycling

Each year, you should review your original plan. Revisit your strategy by reexamining the four critical perspectives identified in the beginning of this chapter, in particular:

♦ Your marketplace
♦ Your competition
♦ Your core capabilities
♦ Your personal definition of success

In fact, as you begin developing a more disciplined approach to managing your business, we recommend that you keep separate files on each of them. Each time you obtain some unique insight into a competitor, for example, document it. That way, the next time you contemplate the firm's future, you'll have a better sense of what you're up against. The same discipline can be applied to the other perspectives. Your clients, your prospects, and your industry contacts will provide you with tremendous insights into each of these areas. What are they thinking and observing, and how does this apply to your practice?

So as you begin the planning cycle each year, be sure to document the elements that will drive future value in your practice and the hurdles you have to overcome. This disciplined approach also allows you to build a history of your business. Such information can be valuable for helping future staff understand the transformation your business has gone through and may offer worthwhile insights for prospective buyers should you ever decide to sell the firm. At the very least, it provides an interesting documentary for you to study someday when you want to reflect on what you've accomplished.

The Value of Surveys

A S ADVISERS STRIVE to build closer relationships with their clients and improve the quality of their services, more firms have begun to formalize their approach to gathering feedback from clients. For advisory firms developing and refining their business strategy, we've found client surveys to be invaluable because they help the firms get in tune with their market and with the services the optimal client looks to them to provide.

For many years, we were skeptical about the value of client surveys because we did not believe that eliciting satisfaction scores from clients would garner anything particularly insightful. It seemed unlikely that clients who disliked an adviser would respond, and those that had "warm and fuzzy" feelings about their advisers would probably sugarcoat their responses. The validity and real value of the client surveys was always suspect to us.

Then we found a survey process that not only allowed clients to evaluate their advisers in a meaningful way but also could be used as a tool to allow clients to identify their needs and preferences in adviser-client communication and the planning areas they wish advisers would address with them. Advisers who participated in such surveys were generally surprised by the results because in many cases they thought they had broached these subjects with their clients, but the overtures had not always registered. Ross Levin, of Accredited Investors, for example, tested a tool developed by Advisor Impact of Toronto. "Our results were positive, and yet some of the specific points were surprising," he says. "Some clients wanted to meet less often than we currently do. Also, some clients wanted more general communication. After the survey, we worked with our staff to determine optimum meeting schedules. We also now send out a regular e-mail update on our views on the market, interest rates, and other relevant data."

Hear No Evil

Despite the potential for such enhancements, only about a third of advisers have surveyed their clients in the last twelve months, according to research by Advisor Impact. And although some advisers point to a lack of time or expertise as the primary obstacles to conducting a survey, the fear factor tends to top the list of self-imposed barriers. Some advisers are afraid to hear what their clients will say—a concern present in both good and bad markets. But research doesn't support the fear factor. Theoretically, in a market as competitive as financial services, existing customers on average tend to be highly satisfied or else they would leave. Our research confirms that argument in practical terms.

As part of a joint venture between Advisor Impact and Moss Adams LLP, we surveyed more than ten thousand clients on behalf of financial advisers across North America. No adviser got an overall satisfaction rating lower than four out of a top score of five. Yet that process also revealed that between 2 percent and 10 percent of clients are, in fact, at risk of defecting. This is a very disturbing percentage considering how many advisers believe their clients are perfectly content. Surveys done in Canada, the United States, and Australia all have identified "managing client expectations" as among the top sources of anxiety for financial advisers. With so many things competing for your time, it's helpful to find efficient tools that allow you to probe these expectations. What's more, in an environment where competition is intensifying and the offerings from banks, CPAs, law firms, and other wealth managers are becoming more responsive, client surveys are a vital intelligence-gathering tool. Your practice may not be geared toward "cross selling" in the traditional sense of a bank or brokerage firm, but retaining clients is a form of selling that every professional adviser must be conscious of. Clearly, a client survey can provide insight beyond what can be gained from regular client contact, because it allows the person to respond without being confronted or having to look the adviser in the eye.

For most advisory firms, more than 85 percent of revenue comes from existing clients. So it's ironic that advisers tend to spend more money on new business development than they do on harvesting and maintaining the relationships they already have. In fact, even compensation plans are geared toward getting more clients rather than retaining or deepening the relationship or share of wallet with current clients.

Client surveys can improve overall client profitability. Properly structured, surveys improve the efficiency, loyalty, time management, and productivity of your professional staff. Systematically uncovering issues through a survey process not only helps you manage costs better; it also makes your practice better able to attract assets, drive revenue, introduce value-added services, and elicit referrals from your client base (see *Figure 3.1*).

A comprehensive study published in the *Harvard Business Review*[1] in 2002 reached some strong conclusions in favor of survey-

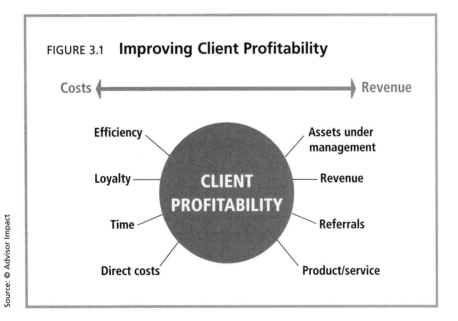

FIGURE 3.1 **Improving Client Profitability**

Costs ⟵————————————⟶ Revenue

Efficiency

Assets under management

Loyalty — **CLIENT PROFITABILITY** — Revenue

Time

Referrals

Direct costs

Product/service

Source: © Advisor Impact

ing clients. The study found that clients surveyed for a large financial institution were more than three times as likely to have opened new accounts, half as likely to have defected, and were more profitable for the firm than clients who were not surveyed. The study noted that these results, which peaked after three months, extended for up to twelve months after the survey.

At least two factors explain these results. First, surveys remind clients that they appreciate the services you offer. In general, clients are unlikely to have spontaneous positive thoughts about you unless reminded or asked explicitly. Second, by asking clients questions about specific services, you increase their awareness of those offerings.

A properly performed client survey will uncover the following:

◆ Satisfaction
◆ Expectations
◆ Preferences
◆ Interests
◆ Referral propensity
◆ Your share of wallet
◆ Client profile

Such insights enhance your value to clients and their value to you.

How to Elicit Constructive Responses

There are three ways to elicit responses from clients: take an ad hoc approach and ask them for comments at the end of a meeting, conduct a telephone survey, or conduct a written survey. To decide which route to take, you'll need to weigh the costs of the program against the depth of information you'll receive and the extent to which answers are provided honestly. In general, written surveys tend to be the best option. Although more expensive, they let you ask a large number of questions, give clients time to respond thoughtfully, and offer clients the option of anonymity.

It can be difficult to directly compare the cost of outsourcing the survey process to the cost of doing it in-house, but you'll typically spend more time and money if you conduct the survey on your own. To create a professional survey instrument with well-designed questions that will yield the insights you seek, you'll likely need to hire a writer and possibly a graphic designer to prepare the questionnaire and then pay for printing and mailing the survey, entering the response data, and analyzing the results. Advisor Impact's Client Audit process, for example, would cost around $2,000 plus outbound postage to survey two hundred households, with an expected 30 percent response rate, but a similar effort done in-house could cost a planner more than twice that amount and likely yield less meaningful results.

Using professional organizations such as Dalbar, Advisor Impact, or local marketing firms tends to enhance the survey process. It's like an individual who prefers to make planning, investment, and risk-management decisions without seeking qualified advice. She can do it cheaper, but can she do it better? We find that advisers who try to do surveys themselves either do not get them finished or have difficulty interpreting the results. Worse yet, they skew the results by asking the wrong questions, or they skew the wording of the questions to get the answers they want to hear.

For the do-it-yourselfer, the first challenge is identifying which questions to ask clients. To start, think beyond "satisfaction." A properly structured survey helps you uncover client expectations, identify cross-selling and consolidation opportunities, pinpoint those clients who are willing to provide referrals, and gather valuable intelligence about any current or planned communications or activities. For the best results, be sure to ask questions in five specific categories:

1. Focus on service satisfaction, both generally and specifically.
2. Probe client expectations regarding contact level.
3. Assess interest in learning about different products and services.
4. Determine client preferences about how you communicate.
5. Ask for profile information to help you populate your database.

Even if you cover all of your bases, not all questions are equally effective. Good questions provide you with specific and targeted

FIGURE 3.2 **What to Ask and How to Ask It**

	Sample Question	Tips and Comments
Satisfaction	My calls are returned promptly (on a five-point scale from "completely agree" to "completely disagree").	Be specific about the elements of client service rather than asking vague questions about service in general.
Expectations	How many times do you expect to meet in a 12-month period to review your financial plan?	Gather quantitative data when possible.
Interests	Which of the following are you interested in learning more about? (Provide list of services.)	Get clients thinking about the services you provide; don't leave too many open-ended questions.
Preferences	Do you think it's important for your financial adviser to provide educational opportunities?	Don't just ask how you are doing; find out what is most important to your clients.
Profile	What is your e-mail address?	Gather better information to populate your database.

information. Bad questions are vague, are difficult to understand, or lead to client responses that are difficult to interpret. (See *Figure 3.2* for examples of good questions in each category.) For every question in a survey, you should know what you'll do with the results. If you do not control client statements at your firm, for example, do not ask about satisfaction with client statements on the survey.

If you do go it alone, the process of surveying clients can be onerous but rewarding. Given the investment of time and money, make sure you fully exploit the results. You can get the biggest bang for your buck by

- ♦ sending a follow-up letter to all clients, highlighting positive feedback and identifying any changes you plan to make as a result of the survey
- ♦ surveying clients every eighteen months and tracking your progress
- ♦ summarizing your results for centers of influence and prospects

Testimonials are helpful, but research data are seen as more objective.

In the spirit of full disclosure, we mention here that Moss Adams LLP adopted the Client Audit process for its advisory-firm clients after evaluating many options. By using a proven survey process—in this case, one developed by Advisor Impact—we've consistently been better able to develop insight into how our advisory-firm clients should be thinking strategically about their businesses.

The Client Audit process is a structured approach that provides a customized solution. The survey form is customized and then provided to the adviser for mailing to clients, and the reports are returned to a central processing center. There, the data are evaluated and interpreted and action steps are developed for the adviser (see *Figure 3.3* on the following page).

In addition to the insight, what's compelling about this process is the action plan that comes out of the survey. So many times, when surveys are performed, clients are often left wondering what the purpose or result was. So regardless of whether you do it on your own or in concert with a professional survey firm, you'll want to translate the survey results into an action step or the process will be wasted, along with the money it cost to do it.

"Since surveying our clients, we've developed a sharper picture of our strengths," says Jennifer Hatch, an adviser with Christopher Street Financial in New York. "We understand our weaknesses and can respond before our clients decide to bail. For example, we were able to understand the level of service that each of our advisers was providing and discovered that [it] varied drastically. As a result, we now set an explicit service standard for everyone in the company."

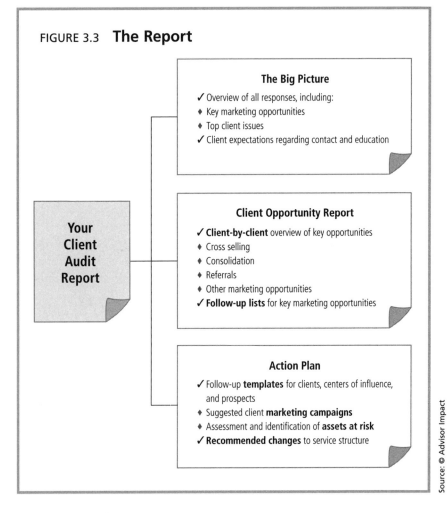

FIGURE 3.3 **The Report**

Your Client Audit Report

The Big Picture
- ✓ Overview of all responses, including:
- ◆ Key marketing opportunities
- ◆ Top client issues
- ✓ Client expectations regarding contact and education

Client Opportunity Report
- ✓ **Client-by-client** overview of key opportunities
- ◆ Cross selling
- ◆ Consolidation
- ◆ Referrals
- ◆ Other marketing opportunities
- ✓ **Follow-up lists** for key marketing opportunities

Action Plan
- ✓ Follow-up **templates** for clients, centers of influence, and prospects
- ◆ Suggested client **marketing campaigns**
- ◆ Assessment and identification of **assets at risk**
- ✓ **Recommended changes** to service structure

Source: © Advisor Impact

Proceed with Caution

You need to be aware of some restrictions regarding how to conduct surveys and how to use the information gathered. The American Marketing Association has a clear code of ethics regarding marketing research, including satisfaction surveys, and that code was written into law. You cannot sell services to clients under the guise of conducting research. Therefore, if you plan to ask questions about client needs and then use that information to follow up with them, make your intentions clear in the cover letter and reiterate that the client may respond anonymously.

Overall, the best way to make a client survey successful is to

♦ keep it short
♦ assess importance and performance
♦ ask actionable questions
♦ include a deadline
♦ provide an incentive
♦ make including client's name optional
♦ code the surveys (to maintain anonymity)
♦ include an open-ended question
♦ make it easy to respond

Client Surveys and the Bottom Line

Many advisers consider client surveys a way to let clients know that they care. They do, in fact, demonstrate a real commitment to client relationships (provided you follow up on the results), but they can do much more.

Our premise throughout this book is that the work of advisers profoundly affects the lives of their clients. An adviser's work gives peace of mind, clears the road to financial independence, and helps individuals and families to manage their risks. Yet many advisers do not have the confidence to ask for fair compensation for the value they provide.

A hidden benefit of the client-survey process is that it allows you to listen and respond constructively to clients in ways that will enhance your value. The survey can provide the psychic gratification of anticipating client needs. But it can also further demonstrate your value to your clients and justify your fees in a way that helps you to be profitable and fairly rewarded for what you provide.

Note

1. Paul M. Kholakia and Vicki G. Morwitz, "How Surveys Influence Customers," *Harvard Business Review* (2002): 18–19.

4. BUILDING LEVERAGE AND CAPACITY

The Challenge of Growth

SINCE THE EMERGENCE of the independent financial adviser in the 1970s, many practitioners in this business have characterized themselves as entrepreneurs. Since they're no longer employees of a parent organization, the notion is that they are, in fact, business owners. They have the same risks and responsibilities as those who leave the cocoon of an employer-based organization and begin their own enterprise. In reality, many of these financial advisers are not entrepreneurs; they are simply self-employed. What's the difference?

Entrepreneurs start a business and build it into an organization that invests in people, systems, and branding. Self-employed advisers, on the other hand, consider themselves employees of their own business, not investors in that business. These firms are operated by individuals who avoid putting money into their business, respond and react to opportunity, and consciously limit growth primarily because they have an aversion or fear of working with other people. That's not to say one approach is better than the other; it's a fork in the road. The right path to take depends on each individual's personal definition of success.

Is this debate merely verbal fencing? Not entirely. By committing to being true entrepreneurs, advisers make a conscious decision to invest in infrastructure that allows them to leverage off of other people, systems, and processes. In other words, they commit to building an enterprise that is not totally dependent on its owner.

That said, the solo practitioner operating simply as someone self-employed is hardly a dead concept. On the contrary, solo practitioners today represent the vast majority of financial advisers and will likely continue to do so. Whether they're operating within a large brokerage house or bank or out of a guest bedroom or garage, many people in this business prefer to work alone rather than be part of a team. Going solo is a lifestyle choice that has merit. These advisers have independence, freedom from having to manage others, and the ability to do as they please without needing anyone else's consent. But the limitations in this model are apparent when you attempt to resolve the competing issues of providing better service to demanding clients, getting access to expertise beyond your own, having the capacity to grow, living a balanced life, and achieving financial independence separate from the business.

The Entrepreneurial Crossroads

The profession is at a crossroads. Will individual practitioners opt for independence rather than depth? Will they struggle to serve clients and grow? Will they be able to respond to the growing need to invest in technology? How dependent will they become on their broker-dealers or custodians to help them build infrastructure? How will this dependence change the economics of their businesses?

Most financial-advisory firms are in that awkward adolescent state. They're too big, yet they're too small. Once an advisory firm begins to add any staff, it has started to accelerate its growth. It will need to monitor and measure performance, coach and counsel people, produce an increasing amount of revenue to cover the added overhead, and invest in more technology solutions, office space, and employee benefits. The joy ride begins, with the owner careening around corners and into dead ends—one foot on the accelerator, the other on the brake.

But most practitioners are consumed by the daily grind. Do you really want to build a business, or would you rather narrow your focus to deal with a few select clients? Although it may be intuitively appealing not to expand your practice so as to avoid the associated headaches, the reality is that every practice will experience problems in each of the management areas much of the time. If you choose not to grow, then you do not provide a career path for the outstanding individuals you hire, which may cause them to leave and in turn force you to hunt for talent again. You may also find it hard to produce sufficient cash flow and profits to reinvest in your business in a way that will help you serve your clients better. And by staying small, you preempt one of the best options for succession. Although you may not be at the point where you're concerned about succession, you can be sure that your clients are. It's likely they've developed some dependence on you, and they surely want to know what will happen to them if something happens to you. Whichever path you choose—growth or no growth—your challenge will always be to provide service and fulfillment to your clients while maintaining an adequate level of income, life balance, and peace of mind in your practice.

Vital Signs

The most successful advisory firms have several common characteristics:

♦ Clear vision and positioning
♦ Human capital aligned with their vision
♦ A compensation plan that reinforces their strategy
♦ A conscious attitude about profit management
♦ A process of systematic client feedback
♦ Built-in leverage and capacity

These concepts apply whether you're a one-person operation or ensemble practice. The difference in the two operating models is that as a solo practitioner, you are the only adviser; in an ensemble model, other advisers or professional staff are a critical part of your practice. We believe that the concepts of strategy, financial management, staffing, and client feedback are relevant and meaningful to solo practitioners, but it has become clear to us that the one thing solo firms lack is the built-in leverage and capacity that distinguishes the elite ensemble firms.

A few years ago, we were asked to look at the team-based platform of a wirehouse that was attempting to move away from the individual-producer model that has always been the operating approach of both insurance and stockbrokerage firms. We were impressed that the teams within this firm were generating more income per adviser and more income per client and seemed to be eliciting higher client-satisfaction scores than their individual-producer counterparts. Granted, this observation had no statistical validity because of the small sample, but it intrigued us enough to examine how independent firms compared.

We sliced the data from our benchmarking studies produced in partnership with the Financial Planning Association (FPA) to evaluate the operating performance of solo practitioners versus ensemble firms. Size did matter among the general population of advisers who opted to become ensemble businesses, meaning they had multiple principals, partners, or professionals (nonowner advisers). The gap was especially startling when we compared the top-performing solo practices with the top-performing ensemble practices. The top-performing ensembles generated almost 20 percent more revenue per professional, nearly twice the revenue per client, and about two times the take-home income per owner than their top-performing solo counterparts (see *Figures 4.1–4.4*).

During the many years of this research, we've continued to observe a gap of some magnitude in key ratios between the two platforms. Anecdotally, advisers who've made the transformation to

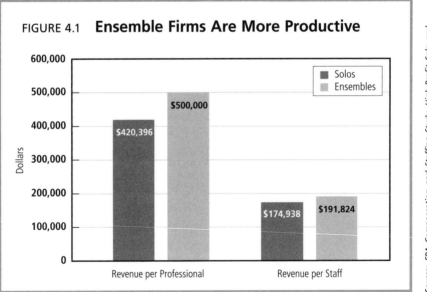

FIGURE 4.1   **Ensemble Firms Are More Productive**

Source: FPA Compensation and Staffing Study, High-Profit Solo and Ensemble Firms, © Moss Adams LLP

Source: FPA Compensation and Staffing Study, High-Profit Solo and Ensemble Firms

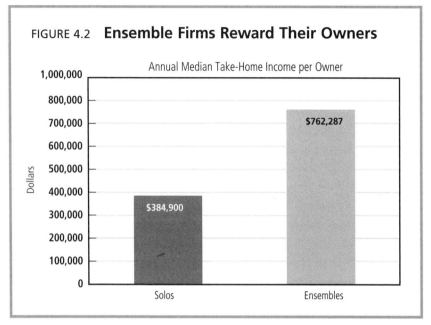

FIGURE 4.2   **Ensemble Firms Reward Their Owners**

Annual Median Take-Home Income per Owner

$384,900 — Solos

$762,287 — Ensembles

Source: © Moss Adams LLP

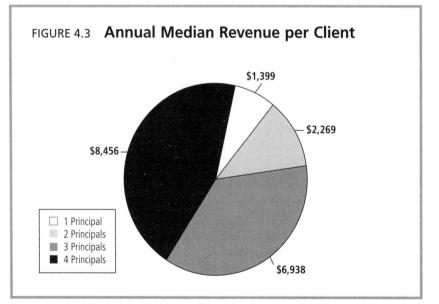

FIGURE 4.3   **Annual Median Revenue per Client**

$1,399

$2,269

$8,456

$6,938

- ☐ 1 Principal
- ☐ 2 Principals
- ☐ 3 Principals
- ■ 4 Principals

the ensemble model tell us that they're more responsive and more proactive in dealing with their clients, which makes sense. In the traditional solo model, the challenge for the adviser is that he or she

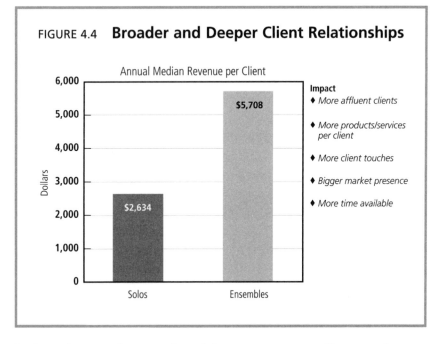

FIGURE 4.4 **Broader and Deeper Client Relationships**

Annual Median Revenue per Client

Impact
♦ More affluent clients
♦ More products/services per client
♦ More client touches
♦ Bigger market presence
♦ More time available

Solos: $2,634
Ensembles: $5,708

Source: FPA Compensation and Staffing Study, High-Profit Solo and Ensemble Firms

is the only one who can give advice, generate new clients, and manage the business. Of course, the administrative staff can support the single owner—and many do so quite well—but they usually do not have the licenses, credentials, interest, skill sets, or qualifications to do what the adviser does (see Figure 4.1).

The Limits of Efficiency

For the solo model, an even more daunting problem relates to profitability: The more clients the firm acquires, the more it needs to add administrative staff to support them. True, certain technology solutions can improve efficiency—see *Virtual-Office Tools for a High-Margin Practice* by David Drucker and Joel Bruckenstein (Bloomberg Press, 2002)—but eventually a practice needs administrative people to deal with the clients. That's what makes this a people business.

When a firm adds administrative staff (this includes management, support staff, and others involved behind the scenes), the cost is charged to overhead expense. In other words, the addition of administrative staff adds nothing to productive capacity. Overhead costs go up while the firm is at a physical limit in terms of how much new business it can take on, because the owner-adviser can manage only a finite number of relationships.

It's becoming more apparent that at least in terms of cost, the level of volume that must be generated in an advisory practice is redefining "critical mass." Critical mass in this context is the point at which a firm is achieving optimal efficiency in its cost structure, optimal profitability based on its client-service model, and optimal effectiveness in the number of clients it can serve well. In terms of effectiveness, the less time an adviser spends dealing with clients, the more sluggish the business becomes and the less valued it is by the clients themselves. In terms of efficiency, advisory firms would ideally keep their overhead costs as a percentage of revenue below 35 percent.

In *Figure 4.5*, we observe what happens to costs as a percentage of revenue as practices grow larger. The data from a study we did of financial-advisory practices for the Financial Planning Association in 2004 shows that expenses as a percentage of revenue actually increased as the firms generated more revenue, peaking at an expense ratio of 44 percent when practices hit $1 million in revenue. The expense ratio declined after that point, as practices

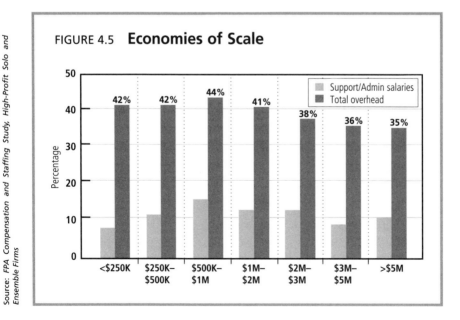

FIGURE 4.5 **Economies of Scale**

Source: FPA Compensation and Staffing Study, High-Profit Solo and Ensemble Firms

became more efficient and added more productive capacity in the form of professional staff. But it isn't until practices hit $5 million of annual revenue that they consistently achieve the optimal expense ratio of 35 percent.

Part of this assessment is obviously theoretical—and, in fact, a flight of fancy for many advisory firms that will never achieve or aspire to a practice this size. But at one time, $1 million of revenue and $100 million of assets under management were considered the ultimate achievement. Now it appears that $5 million is the new level of critical mass for an advisory firm. The challenge is to determine how many clients, generating how much in fees, served by how many advisers will a firm need to achieve critical mass by this definition? And what are the implications for the client-service approach and for the infrastructure if the practice grows to this size?

Time Well Spent?

Julie Littlechild at Advisor Impact offers a way to come up with an answer to this question. Littlechild examined how much time a typical adviser spends serving high-priority clients, average clients, and low-priority clients. *Figure 4.6* shows that advisers clearly max out in terms of the number of optimal relationships they can manage. Let's look at the time spent serving the high-priority clients.

In this example, an adviser estimates he has eleven proactive contacts with each high-priority client in a year—three face-to-face meetings and eight by phone. Each of these meetings requires some preparation. The adviser also consumes a fair amount of time responding to client inquiries, which often involve some research as well. The total time spent dealing with a high-priority client is estimated at 19.8 hours per year. For the sake of simplicity, let's round this to twenty hours.

The typical adviser puts in 1,800 hours in an average work year—some work more, some less. By dividing twenty hours into 1,800, it would appear that the maximum number of high-priority clients the adviser can manage is ninety. And that's assuming the adviser does nothing else and that he has only top-priority clients. Of course, that's never the case, which makes this exercise all the more painful for advisers who have no way to leverage.

FIGURE 4.6   **Contact Goal: Senior Adviser**

	Face to Face	Telephone	Proactive Contacts/Year
Top-Priority Clients	3	8	11
Average Clients	2	4	6
Low-Priority Clients	1	2	3

What if the adviser added associate-level professional staff who could handle client meetings and respond to client needs and were properly trained and licensed to provide advice? What if he invested in technology and other tools that would allow him to leverage better? Would these changes allow him to grow more profitably and be even more responsive to client issues?

Assuming the adviser has already implemented technology solutions to become very efficient, he now has few methods by which to grow the firm's income: cull the clients to remove the ones at the bottom and take on only the more profitable relationships, limit the number of clients the firm takes on so that he can keep the administrative staff at a manageable size, or raise his fees. If he does any of these things, he probably can preserve the firm's size and maintain his span of control over a key number of client relationships. But advisers typically do not recognize that they're drowning in opportunity until they're overwhelmed. None of these remedies directly addresses the client-service problems he may have created by growing beyond his ability to provide clients with good service, but these steps can at least keep relationship management within reach.

Each of these choices is reasonable, but they're likely to go against the grain for advisers who thrive on new clients or those who feel an obligation to respond to their sources of referral when new business opportunities come in. This point was brought home to us in a study group of ten advisers. Twice a year, they would meet to share successes and challenges, compare their firms' numbers and ratios, and take turns making presentations on new initiatives. At one of the meetings, one adviser was adamant that he had no desire to grow his firm beyond its present size. "Look," he said, "I make a good living, I have time to spend with my kids while they're young, and I'm able to tend to my clients' needs." Surprisingly, when his turn came later in the meeting to present a new initiative, he rolled out a very aggressive marketing program in alliance with a local certified public accountant and law firm, which was producing great numbers of new opportunities. His fellow study group members eagerly pointed out the contradiction between this plan and his desire not to grow. Chastened, he said, "I guess I'm just addicted to growth."

He became even more uncomfortable when the group looked over his financial data. They saw a tremendous increase in overhead expenses as a percentage of revenue, especially in the categories of marketing and administrative salaries (and related expenses, such as benefits). He also told the group that he was looking for more space to accommodate his fleet of support staff. He later admitted that it was getting harder for him to tend to his clients while having to manage a growing number of staff who were not directly involved in the advisory cycle but were hired primarily to support him.

This example points out one of the biggest hurdles for advisers who choose to work alone, at least in terms of managing both costs and lifestyle. The solo model works extraordinarily well for those who do not want to grow, but for many advisers, that's a little like a heroin addict not wanting a fix. There are exceptions, but the law of professional practices is that once you become known for being really good, everybody wants to do business with you. And it's very hard to turn away good clients. Furthermore, it seems that for many advisers, the concept of working alone applies only to other professional staff, not to support staff. Consequently, they have all the headaches of adding people without the benefits of including other professionals who could challenge them, give depth to their practice, and be another source of revenue and profits for the business.

So, if you're addicted to growth, is there a more practical way to become an elite practice? Yes.

Cornerstones of the Professional Practice

As elite firms have discovered, building an organization that has the professional capacity to help manage relationships and extend the enterprise often brings more reward than pain. Without growth, it's almost impossible to provide a career path for staff members. Without a career path, it's almost impossible to recruit, develop, and retain excellent staff. And without excellent staff, it's almost impossible to build capacity and create operating leverage in a practice. Ensemble models provide an opportunity to do all of this: handle growth, offer career development, and create leverage—the cornerstones of every professional practice.

Growing Concerns

Of course, there are legitimate concerns about whether growth can work for you, such as:

♦ Rising costs
♦ Loss of management control
♦ Loss of quality control
♦ Client satisfaction
♦ Training staff that may later become your competitors

But these threats exist whether you grow or not. Let's break them down.

Cost. A key concept to keep in mind is the difference between operating profit and gross profit. If your gross profit margin is declining, it's likely to be due to one of five factors: poor pricing, poor productivity, poor payout, poor product or service mix, or poor client mix. If your operating profit margin is declining, any of three factors might be involved: reduced gross profit, insufficient revenue volume to support your infrastructure, or poor cost control.

Since we began in the mid-1980s to benchmark the financial performance of financial-advisory firms, we've observed that overhead costs as a percentage of revenue have been steadily increasing, even in good markets. The three fastest-rising costs have been rent, salaries, and payroll-related expenses like benefits. And these costs have been increasing at a faster rate than revenue has, making the trend even more alarming.

Apparently, skyrocketing office-rental rates were only part of the reason this category was seeing a spike. The biggest driver turned out to be additions in square footage to accommodate the growing support staff of many practices and the desire of many advisers to be housed in more impressive quarters. But the addition of staff by itself is not a negative. The negative is the relationship of staff costs to revenue and revenue to total staff. When practices add overhead costs without adding productive capacity, it's logical that their profit margins will suffer. So if the squeeze is on anyway, why not add professional staff who will add productive capacity and not costs alone?

Loss of management control. The extent of control is a legitimate problem for any business, regardless of size. It appears that practices hit the wall managerially when they grow to eight people, then again at fifteen, and again at twenty-five to thirty. It's as if the communication links get disconnected and the management process breaks down. Advisers in all firms, but especially smaller firms, are at a disadvantage when this happens, because they have no one to whom they can delegate key responsibilities. Larger practices need to build in structure to manage and communicate effectively.

Loss of quality control. As with management control, the increasing size of the business may cause the owner and lead adviser to lose touch with much of what's going on. But most advisers tell us that they're concerned about what may be falling through the cracks anyway. The absence of protocols to manage client relationships simply makes the problem more glaring as the practice gets bigger and attracts more clients. These protocols are critical regardless of the size of the business to ensure clients are served and work is done consistently.

Client satisfaction. The linkage continues with client satisfaction. In a firm headed by an adviser who has little time to manage the business and serve existing clients and whose grip on quality control is loosening, client interaction and consequently client satisfaction are likely to suffer. Remaining small does not prevent this, although having competent administrative staff to tend to clients does help. Limiting the number of active client relationships per professional staff enhances your chances of having fulfilled clients. But putting a limit on relationships also puts a limit on growth if there is no one else in the firm able to deal with the new clients.

Training your competitors. It seems that the No. 1 reason solo practitioners do not want to add professional staff is because they fear that by training them and giving them access to the firm's clients, they're spawning new competitors with an insider's edge. Of all the concerns about a firm's growth, this one is the hardest to resolve, because ambitious people usually do want to have their own businesses. Yet we've seen many examples of firms that have provided a legitimate career path, including the opportunity for ownership or partnership, and consequently have retained outstanding people to help the business develop. This is the model used successfully by other professional service firms such as accountants and attorneys. Through the use of restrictive legal agreements, the firms are also usually able to protect their client base from poaching by a disaffected former employee or partner. Even better, through the deliberate development of a career path and human-capital plan, the firms are able to create skilled professionals who see as much or more opportunity inside the firm as they do outside.

These issues arise regardless of a firm's size. They show up in different ways in a solo practice, but they do exist to some degree. The elite firms have recognized these pressures and have structured their organizations to use size to their advantage instead of battling them from a position of weakness.

Models That Work

Every business needs a vision, a strategy, a framework for making decisions about the clients it serves, how it serves them, and what services to offer. The model for a business focused on the 401(k) market, for example, will look dramatically different from a wealth-management practice geared to the ultrawealthy. A financial-planning business will also look very different from a pure investment-management firm or one that's predominantly an insurance agency or brokerage.

But assuming your practice is not product-oriented and instead focuses on clients' needs, you can broaden your organization once you've defined the optimal clients and the service experience best suited to them. For the purpose of this discussion, we'll use as our model a wealth-management practice that offers clients comprehensive financial solutions. Elite practices positioned as wealth-management firms have two common structures: the multidisciplinary model and the leveraged model.

The Multidisciplinary Model

The multidisciplinary model entails an integrated combination of skills that allows advisers to take a more comprehensive approach to the financial lives of their clients. Financial advisers of this type are usually relationship managers and have surrounded themselves with experts in relevant areas such as risk management, investment management, financial planning, and estate planning (see *Figure 4.7*). Of course, the disciplines represented on the team depend on the business's strategy and the predominant needs of the clients served. For example, if your optimal clients are business owners in transition, you may need to surround yourself with experts in management succession or family dynamics to assist with the emotional issues that inevitably arise. If your optimal clients are dentists, you might include on your team experts in dental-practice management, since this is such an important part of the clients' wealth creation.

The point is that you work from the client in, rather than the service out. Using a client survey process, as described in chapter 3, you can begin to define the expectations and needs of your optimal client.

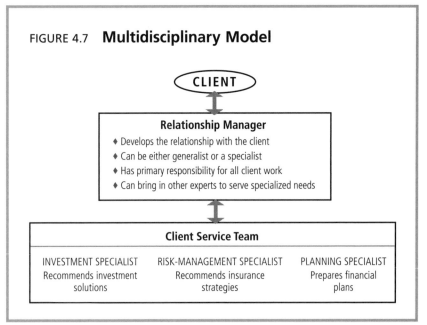

FIGURE 4.7   **Multidisciplinary Model**

CLIENT

Relationship Manager
♦ Develops the relationship with the client
♦ Can be either generalist or a specialist
♦ Has primary responsibility for all client work
♦ Can bring in other experts to serve specialized needs

Client Service Team

INVESTMENT SPECIALIST	RISK-MANAGEMENT SPECIALIST	PLANNING SPECIALIST
Recommends investment solutions	Recommends insurance strategies	Prepares financial plans

Source: © Moss Adams LLP

The limitation of the multidisciplinary model is that it provides fewer opportunities for development of career paths. Typically, specialists stay within that role rather than evolving to primary relationship managers. Although this route may be acceptable to them, the challenge for you is to develop enough relationship managers to help you grow and attract more primary client relationships.

Some multidisciplinary practices create multiple teams that are all relationship-oriented, then either outsource the specialties or treat the specialists as staff positions. From an organizational perspective, this means that the line positions (the advisers and relationship managers) focus on selling and serving clients; the staff positions (the technical specialists) focus on supporting the advisers and relationship managers. This is an effective way to leverage your business as well.

The Leveraged Model

The variation diagrammed in *Figure 4.8* seems to be the strongest model in terms of driving growth and building capacity, leverage, expertise, and client focus. We call this the leveraged model.

In the leveraged model, the senior financial advisers play a strategic role in client service, while the associates (or junior advisers) serve

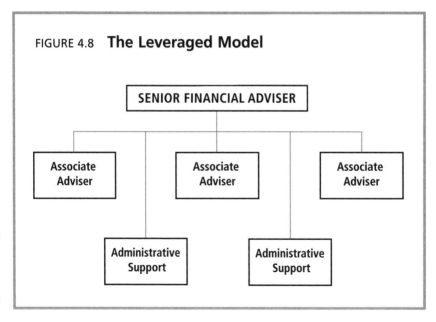

FIGURE 4.8 **The Leveraged Model**

SENIOR FINANCIAL ADVISER

Associate Adviser

Associate Adviser

Associate Adviser

Administrative Support

Administrative Support

Source: © Moss Adams LLP

a tactical role. The senior financial adviser develops new business and leads discussions about critical planning and implementation decisions that the client must make. The associate implements the plans and is the primary day-to-day contact with the client.

We've found that wealth managers operating alone can effectively manage between sixty and ninety primary relationships; pure investment-management firms may not be able to manage as many relationships if they have numerous accounts per client, but each firm can define the number for itself. In either case, by building out the leveraged model, the team is able to manage two to three times more client relationships than an adviser working alone.

This approach also provides the context for a career path. For example, a professional staff member can come in as an analyst or a planner, rise to the next level of senior analyst or senior planner, then to financial adviser, and ultimately to senior financial adviser. These are just suggested titles, but the idea is that the roles and expectations, and therefore the compensation, changes at each level. Upon mastering one level, an employee is eligible to be promoted to the next, providing the firm's economics and business needs support this.

In either the leveraged model or the multidisciplinary model, clients belong to the business, not to the individual advisers. Each staff person should be asked to sign a restrictive covenant agreement, which recognizes this fact and protects the firm against the possibility of its members hijacking clients. The team approach also helps protect the adviser against defectors, because the client relationships run deep and broad and are not tied to a single individual.

Compensation to the participants in the team—especially the professional staff—should be a combination of base salary plus incentives. Base compensation will rise for the members as their responsibilities, experience, credentials, and contributions increase. Incentives should be tied to team success and individual performance, revolving around critical benchmarks such as client satisfaction, revenue per client, profit per client, and gross profit margin of the team.

It's important for leaders of such teams not to assign low-priority clients to the associates. A decision should be made about which clients you'll serve and why, and the whole team should be focused on serving optimal clients. Each client will have a manager and a co-manager, with the associate serving in the latter role. It is prudent in this model to stagger the associates in terms of years of experience—for example, one to three years, three to five years, and five to seven years. This allows you to gradually build internal successors and involve others in the development of their juniors. This process also provides you with an opportunity to observe how your associates are evolving as leaders and managers. The different levels of experience and tenure also provide for a natural progression in their development. That is not to say that an analyst could not leap frog the financial adviser in the career progression, but if done right, the staff becomes almost like a laddered portfolio.

The downside of this model is that it tends to involve a higher level of fixed costs in the beginning, especially costs related to staffing and infrastructure. But that is the power of leverage. Once you break even, your return over and above labor costs goes up exponentially. The basic difference is that solo owners can get a reward only for their own labor; in the ensemble model, owners can get a return for other people's labor as well. This is not to say the ensemble model is exploitative. In fact, it's entrepreneurial because you're leveraging resources—in this case, human resources—to add value for your clients while at the same time focusing on your own unique abilities.

Implementing the Leveraged Model

Every business plan begins with a vision. Where do you want to be five years from now? What type of organization will you need to build to achieve these goals? What are the gaps in your business between now and then? What specific, measurable action steps must you take to close these gaps?

Begin by evaluating your organization, then deciding which strategic framework is best for you. This means defining the optimal client and the client-service experience. Once that's clear, it will be easier to define the positions that must be staffed and the other resource commitments that must be made.

From there, you can build your economic model. If you know, for example, that you want to keep your direct expenses at 40 percent of revenue and your overhead expenses at 35 percent of revenue, you will be able to build a model that tells you how much revenue you need, generated by how many clients at a certain level, who get a certain level of service.

To help you determine the compensation for different staff positions, the best resource in the wealth-management business is the compensation and staffing survey published by the Financial Planning Association (FPA) every other year (www.fpanet.org). This is a good foundation on which to build your economic model to determine what it will take for you to achieve critical mass.

Leveraging Your Affiliations

Successful advisory practices also leverage their affiliations with broker-dealers, custodians, or turnkey providers. In fact, these connections could be among an adviser's most important strategic relationships. However, we have found that far too many advisers take a very narrow view of these relationships by thinking of them only in terms of cost. Yet, if you look closely at these businesses, you'll find that each has a unique value proposition, a unique culture, and a specific attitude about how it supports its advisers. One support system isn't necessarily better than another; each is simply different. To maximize the efficiency and the potential of your firm, you should always select a custodian or broker-dealer in the context of your strategy—that is, in terms of which organization best supports what you're trying to accomplish.

Affiliation Model

Advisers often allow their backgrounds to dictate their affiliations, rather than making a conscious choice about what would be best for them and their practice. There are, in fact, a number of affiliation models in this industry and a number of choices for advisers to make regarding which model on the continuum will best help them implement their own business strategies. *Figure 4.9* depicts the affiliation model spectrum as we see it.

Many advisers came into the business as salespeople by way of the traditional securities brokerage or general agency system. We refer to that platform as one of complete control. Brokerage firms such as Merrill Lynch and Morgan Stanley best represent this model, as

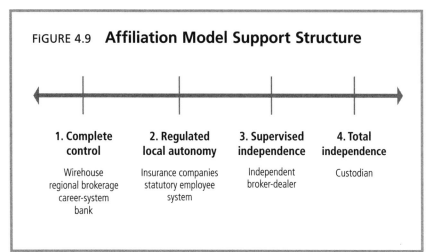

FIGURE 4.9   **Affiliation Model Support Structure**

1. Complete control	2. Regulated local autonomy	3. Supervised independence	4. Total independence
Wirehouse regional brokerage career-system bank	Insurance companies statutory employee system	Independent broker-dealer	Custodian

Source: © Moss Adams LLP

do general agency systems such as Northwestern Mutual and bank financial-services networks such as Wells Fargo or Wachovia. Many advisers have built dynamic practices within this framework and have leveraged off the brand recognition that these parent firms provide. The primary advantage of this platform is the cocoon it offers, enabling advisers to focus on their clients and defer most business issues to the parent firm. These advisers generally receive a high level of support, and the firms typically have a significant identity and presence in a local market. The downside is usually the inability to build a salable practice, which significantly limits how these advisers can run their business affairs, the products they can offer, and some-times even how they can interact with clients. And the portion of the revenues they get to keep is also often quite a bit less than they'd get under other affiliation models, in direct relationship to the increased number of services offered by these platforms.

Of course, a significant number of advisers have migrated to one of the other three types of affiliation: regulated local autonomy, supervised independence, and total independence. Each of these models has its own set of advantages and challenges. As a rule, the farther you break away from a completely controlled environment, the higher the payout. But advisers in these other platforms are also more responsible for their costs, infrastructure, and technical sup-port. In other words, independence comes with a cost.

A good example of this migration is the system in place at American Express Financial Advisors in Minneapolis, which offers three affiliation platforms that mirror typical industry models: Platform I is indeed completely controlled, and advisers who choose this model become employees of the firm; Platform II is for statutory employees, who are then responsible for their own business expenses; and Platform III is for independent contractors, who no longer operate under the American Express name but who use an affiliated firm as their broker-dealer.

Raymond James Financial in St. Petersburg, Florida, is another example of a once-traditional broker-dealer that now crosses all four of the possible platforms with its Adviser Select initiative. In this instance, the mix is slightly different, offering relationships with its full-service brokerage firm, its independent broker-dealer, and a totally independent institutional-services platform.

In the early 1990s, discount broker Charles Schwab & Co. in San Francisco changed the broker-dealer model with its then-revolutionary institutional-services division. Many advisers discarded their broker-dealer affiliations, in some cases relinquishing their securities licenses, and set up custodial relationships with Schwab Institutional. Companies such as Fidelity Registered Investment Adviser Group in Boston, T.D. Waterhouse Institutional in New York, and DataLynx in Denver have also become significant players in this market, offering their advisers total independence in product selection, business affairs, and client relationships, along with 100 percent of the revenues those relationships generate. Certain turnkey providers of asset-management services, such as SEI Investments, BAM Advisor Services LLC, and the Frank Russell Co., have also, in some respects, supplemented the broker-dealer relationship.

A more recent evolution has been the creation of independent trust companies, which a number of fee-based advisers are looking to use as custodians and to clear securities at lower costs to their clients without the perceived threat of competition from their affiliation partner. The trust company model also may potentially fall under the jurisdiction of banking regulators rather than securities regulators, which can provide clients a higher degree of comfort.

Implications for Advisers

Any one of these four platforms can be an appropriate choice, depending on an adviser's individual business strategy. In some cases, being a local representative of a national brand is an effective way to attract and serve clients without a large investment in business infrastructure. Traditionally, this has been the way most advisers enter the business. The catch, of course, is that the payout in the standardized platform is not as high as in the alternative channels, and there may be more pressure to advocate for the company's own products or for outside products in which the parent company has an interest.

The regulated local autonomy model also is an appealing platform for those looking for some of the best characteristics of a wirehouse or general agency cocoon, but with some degree of independence regarding product, service, and brand name. Payouts are typically higher in this system than under the complete control model but not at the same level of supervised independence. The simple reason is that most independent broker-dealers cannot afford to provide as much infrastructure and still sustain their high payouts to advisers. The rule of thumb is that the more support you need, the less payout you get to keep. It's a matter of purchasing support and infrastructure from your strategic partner or creating it on your own. That balance shifts as you move along the continuum of control versus independence.

The supervised independence model is quite appealing to independent advisers, provided they have the ability and interest to manage their practices and resources effectively. Payouts for an independent broker-dealer generally range between 65 and 90 percent and average 85 percent. This platform tends to impose fewer controls on its advisers, but in fact it only works for advisers who are emotionally and managerially ready to grow their own businesses without a safety net. It's also an appealing option for those who have expanded their fee-based business but still have a substantial amount of trailing commissions from mutual fund sales that they would be reluctant or economically unable to leave on the table under a total independence model.

The total independence model provides a great amount of flexibility and advantage for advisers who operate in the fee-only market.

Not only do these advisers collect fees in a wholly owned business entity (NASD rules prohibit commissions to be paid to a business unless it's registered as a broker-dealer), they collect 100 percent of what they charge. If they're effective in managing their practices, comfortable asking for appropriate fees, and willing to take full responsibility for their own compliance supervision, this model is very compelling. The risk is that advisers using this platform are walking a tightrope without a net. They need to be much more effective business managers, and they must appreciate that the level of support simply is not going to be as great as it is in the other three platforms.

Relevance to Practice Management

The firm an adviser chooses as a business affiliate will affect the practice's strategy, compensation, personnel choices, and financial results. Each platform has appeal, depending on what you feel you can do well, what you need a partner to do—and what your personal goals are. As you develop your strategy, examine which model best suits your business. If you do not have the time, money, and management capability to undertake an initiative on your own, consider how each of these firms would help you to fulfill your goals. They are sources of products, technology, advanced-planning education, contacts, acquisition and succession assistance, client referrals, and more.

For some practices, the payout may become the overriding reason to affiliate with one firm rather than another. But often this is a shortsighted approach. Remember that the higher the payout, the fewer dollars the affiliate has available to invest in infrastructure to support you. There are many opportunities to leverage the resources of larger organizations to build your business today and reap greater rewards in the future. The key is to make sure the trade-off you make is the right one for you. It all depends on what you need and where you want to go. Your argument should never be about payout percentages but about dollars. Which platform can allow you to achieve the return on investment and the growth in revenue that you consider key to your firm's future value?

Human Capital

WHEN I WAS A younger man, I was appointed chief executive officer of a small business by my partners. This seemed to be a natural step in my ascendancy to management glory. After all, I liked people, I had spent many years learning to be a follower, and I certainly knew the deficiencies in the current leadership.

Reality struck a short time later, when all the employees turned out to be subversive enemies of the company, committed to undermining authority, profits, and the firm's stated commitment to client service. Any semblance of a work ethic had obviously evaporated among this younger generation. And the older employees seemed to be marking their time. My staff's apparent complacency was making me furious. "Off with their heads," I'd scream at my partners, who'd smirk like Mona Lisa, amused that Mr. Nice Guy could turn out to be just as jaded a capitalist as they were. "What if we got rid of these employees and all this management crap," I asked in a moment of inspiration, "so we could focus on clients? It's obvious that nobody is going to understand this business the way we do. We've already proved we can do it better ourselves anyway."

That's when the questions came flying: "How will the business grow without employees? How will going it alone help us serve clients better? Or develop new services? Or build value? Or make more money? What kind of a strategy is that? Are you nuts?"

So my ebullience changed to depression, then deeper depression. How had I gotten into this mess? All I'd ever really wanted to do was to build my client base and give life-altering advice to those who hired me. Who knew that running a business could be so hard? I reflected on a question posed by a motivational speaker I'd once heard, "How many of you dreamed of owning a boat?" he asked the audience. Nods and amens followed. Then he asked, "How many of you remember if the dream included cleaning the boat?" That said it all.

The Problem You Can't Do Without

Obviously, this tongue-in-cheek saga is meant to make a point. It's very hard for many who run small businesses not to take things personally. In movies and books, business owners are ruthless and tightfisted. In reality, business owners have feelings of insecurity, emotional peaks and valleys, and tremendous anxiety because they have so much at stake. It's hard to make constructive, logical decisions when you witness behavior that puts your business at risk.

Owners and managers of advisory firms the world over may recognize this epiphany. The small-business guru Michael E. Gerber observed in his book *The E Myth Revisited: Why Most Small Businesses Don't Work and What to Do About It* (HarperBusiness, 1995) that most entrepreneurs don't start in business because they dream of being a business owner. They start because they have some technical skill and the business is kind of a necessary evil for making money with that skill. In fact, the business evolves naturally, until it becomes a complex, living organism.

The same is true in the advisory industry and in the evolution of most advisory firms. In Moss Adams's first study for the Financial Planning Association on staffing and compensation within financial-advisory firms, we asked the participating firms what their top ten challenges were. Five of them had to do with human capital:

1. Time management
2. Efficiency
3. Capacity
4. Hiring staff
5. Managing growth

Whether intended or not, most financial-advisory firms grow their business to the point where they need additional staff to respond adequately to clients. The challenge for the adviser is finding and keeping good people. Without quality staff, time management, efficiency, growth, and the capacity to serve clients all suffer. These are the symptoms of a firm that lacks a coherent plan for selecting, managing, and rewarding their staff.

A whole science has evolved to study the issues of managing and developing staff. Financial-advisory firms are like little test labs, where common problems and solutions occur daily. The evolution of your human-capital strategy will take time, but the investment will produce returns well beyond what you could accomplish alone. And once constructed and implemented, it will fulfill you as an entrepreneur.

Aligning Human Capital with Strategy

The most critical concept in the development of your human-capital plan is ensuring its alignment with your business's strategic plan. In chapter 2 we discussed how to develop a strategy for your business. Again, your strategy is the confluence of choices that will allow you to

◆ build on your current capabilities
◆ position your firm against your competitors
◆ respond to the external market
◆ fulfill your personal definition of success

This business strategy must drive your human-capital strategy. As with many tactical areas, advisers tend to make human-capital decisions in a reactionary or opportunistic way, as opposed to strategically and in support of their long-term vision. This strategic alignment is critical at even the most basic level of human-capital planning—deciding whether or not you will *have* staff other than yourself in your organization. Your business strategy will drive this decision.

One adviser recently told us that instead of hiring other people and building a larger organization, she plans to focus on her unique ability, which is advising clients, not managing staff. This is a viable approach for some business strategies, and it's the right choice for her if she can overcome its challenges and if it allows her to implement her business strategy. But when we asked her how she intended to differentiate her firm in her market (that is, her business strategy), she told us she wants to be known as the dominant provider of wealth-management services to widows in Southern California— a viable strategy but one that requires significant resources, including human resources. Her "dominance" business strategy will at some point need to come into line with her "minimalist" human-capital strategy—and one or the other will have to give. Dominance, or meaningful growth, typically implies the addition of staff and the development of a human-capital plan in line with that business strategy.

Most advisers do not dream of the opportunity to recruit and manage people. They prefer to work with clients. But those who choose to grow their organization and build their team recognize that it can be just as valuable, if not more so, to give their staff the same attention they do clients. This is how they truly discover the power of organizational leverage—creating a business that draws on more than just their own personal time and resources.

The human-capital plan, therefore, can be as critical to the business as the strategic plan is. It must be aligned with the strategic plan, but it's far more tactical in nature. Which clients you serve and which services and products you offer—core elements of your business strategy—will dictate the critical staff positions for your business and the type of individuals you hire to fill those positions. Once your strategy is developed, envision what this will mean for the business five years hence:

♦ How many clients do you hope to serve and in what form?
♦ How many clients can be served by an individual adviser or by a team of advisers?
♦ What type of administrative and technological support will be required to make the advisers effective in their roles?
♦ What will be the job descriptions for each of these positions?
♦ What will optimum performance look like for each job?

If your business strategy focuses on a particular niche, for instance, then your first task is to identify the critical characteristics of the optimal client base and attempt to project the issues that will affect these clients during the next one to five years. The answers help you identify which products and services you will offer to help those target clients and address their needs, as well as identify how best to deliver these services and products and which professional and support positions you will need to add to do so.

Case Study: The Hutch Group

GLEN AND LAUREL are partners in the Hutch Group, a firm whose strategic vision is to be known for serving business owners in transition. It's a niche firm focused on a specific market. To create their human-capital plan, Glen and Laurel begin by evaluating the needs of their target market, then assessing what jobs and functions they require within the firm and the type of individuals they need to hire. They set out to determine the **nature of the work,** the **nature of the worker,** and the **nature of the workplace** at the Hutch Group.

They look first at the key characteristics and trends with respect to business owners in transition.

Characteristics

♦ They have a high net worth but are not yet liquid.
♦ Forty percent to 80 percent of their net worth is tied up in the business.
♦ They have management-succession and ownership-succession issues.
♦ They have estate-planning issues to address.
♦ They may be on their second family.
♦ They may not be emotionally ready to leave the business.

Future Trends

♦ Changes in estate tax laws may affect their transition options.
♦ Their industry may be going through consolidation or contraction.
♦ Children are increasingly deciding not to go into their parents' businesses.
♦ A large percentage of business leaders are within five years of retirement.

The Hutch Group's Human-Capital Response to the Market

GLEN AND LAUREL evaluate these characteristics and trends to determine the nature of the work in their organization and what capabilities they need to employ. Understanding these trends and their implications for how the Hutch Group needs to prepare to serve these clients in the future, Glen and Laurel decide the firm will need to develop capabilities in estate planning, management-succession planning, ownership-transition planning, and business planning as complements to its current offering in personal financial planning.

Since it's unlikely any one individual can master all of these disciplines, these additional services dictate the type of individuals the Hutch Group will need to add to staff. By examining these needs, they can now define the nature of the workers they need. They set out to define the individual characteristics and skill sets needed for each job to fulfill their clients' requirements. They define the key desirable characteristics related to skills, abilities, motivations, and interests and decide they need to hire individuals who are

♦ analytical
♦ persuasive
♦ planning oriented
♦ skilled at communication
♦ eager to work with more complex situations
♦ able to work easily with concepts, data, and numbers

In addition to finding candidates matched to the job, Glen and Laurel must also focus on the nature of the workplace—creating an environment in which these individuals will flourish. The business strategy they've defined—particularly their personal definitions of success and desire to build a business beyond their own personal time and reputations—requires that they create an organization that offers an opportunity for career growth, intellectual challenge, personal development, individual coaching, meaningful interactions with clients, and appropriate financial rewards.

As illustrated in the case study, your business strategy will drive the three distinct but interrelated elements of your human capital plan:

1. The nature of the work
2. The nature of the worker
3. The nature of the workplace (see chapter 6, "The Care and Preening of Staff")

The Nature of the Work

The most important thing you can do to ensure you are making good strategic hires is to ensure that the work—every function in the organization—is being driven by a business need. Don't begin your planning with a "must-have" candidate or a "do-have" employee, but rather with an understanding of what the business needs.

Defining the Business Needs

To pinpoint the needs of the practice you're building, ask yourself these questions:

♦ What is my business strategy? What do I want the business to be known for?
♦ What target clients and target services and products does that strategy necessarily include?
♦ What do I want the client experience to be like?
♦ What specific job functions need to be in place to offer those services and products to those clients in that way?

Begin with a mental clean slate and build your organization without regard to names so that you are not handicapped by pre-conceptions. This approach will allow you to construct a framework in which your current staff can either fit or not. One of the biggest mistakes small-business owners make is trying to fit the organization to the people it employs, instead of the other way around.

Defining the Job

When Moss Adams conducted its first FPA Compensation and Staffing Survey, we were shocked by how poorly defined the positions were in most firms. In fact, there was virtually no consistency in definitions and expectations across practices. This hodgepodge is symptomatic of an immature industry and makes the management of staff a bigger challenge than it should be. A fundamental rule of business management tells us to define the roles, expectations, and accountability for each job so that we know what to evaluate and how to manage performance improvement.

Multitasking is a concept long applied to owning and working for a small business. Many entrepreneurs treat their staff as if they were human fodder and just keep throwing bodies at the problem in the hope of overwhelming their enemy, much the way the generals fighting ancient wars did. Not much thought is given to what the specific task is. As a result, it's difficult to measure a staff's success.

Each job requires a different set of characteristics. That makes it essential to define the nature of the job, how success will be measured, and the qualities required to fulfill the job well. The priorities of a job must be clearly spelled out so that the staff knows which issues take precedent when interests and priorities collide.

Depending on your strategy and client-service experience, jobs may need to be defined in the areas of

♦ sales and marketing
♦ client service
♦ operations
♦ compliance
♦ investment advice and management
♦ risk analysis and management
♦ financial planning
♦ estate planning
♦ tax planning

The *FPA Compensation and Staffing Study* defines jobs in a number of categories, as outlined below (see "Job Responsibilities"). Some of these positions are more likely to be full-time jobs in larger firms but may be just a part of someone's job in a smaller firm. For that reason, the study categorizes the jobs by function. A "job" may ultimately be composed of multiple "functions." Your firm may have

Job Responsibilities

Management Functions

◆ **President, CEO, managing partner:** Provides strategic concepts, planning, and broad executive management to achieve the firm's strategic objectives. This is a purely managerial function, with no responsibility for producing revenue.

◆ **General manager, COO, director of operations:** Directs, administers, and coordinates the activities of the organization in accordance with policies, goals, and objectives established by the owner(s). This is a purely managerial function, with no responsibility for producing revenue.

◆ **CFO, controller:** Establishes policies and procedures for effective recording, analyzing, and reporting of all financial matters of the organization.

◆ **Human resources director:** Primarily responsible for staffing, recruiting, training, determining compensation strategy, policies, and procedures.

◆ **Compliance officer:** Responsible for developing and monitoring the firm's compliance program, ensuring that all activities meet the requirements of state and federal legal and regulatory agencies; acts as liaison with regulatory agencies on compliance-related issues in response to complaints.

Senior Professional Functions

◆ **Senior financial planner, senior financial adviser:** Primarily responsible for financial planning and delivery of financial advice, with extensive client contact and client-relationship management.

◆ **Investment adviser:** Primarily responsible for delivery of investment advice, with extensive client contact and client-relationship management.

◆ **Investment manager, portfolio manager:** Services clients' investment portfolios in accordance with their investment goals; responsible for investment policy, buying and selling decisions, and asset allocation; may also be responsible for technology and trading.

◆ **Tax planner, estate planner:** Primarily responsible for consulting with clients on various tax and/or estate issues; may be a CPA.

◆ **Business-development specialist** ("rainmaker"): Primarily responsible for sales and marketing; possibly responsible for some client management, but main focus is business development.

Support Functions

◆ **Junior financial planner, junior financial adviser, paraplanner:** A technical position responsible for the detail work in developing modular or comprehensive financial plans for clients in support of a relationship manager; limited client contact except in meetings, data gathering, and follow-up.

◆ **Tax preparer:** Prepares tax returns for clients; limited client contact except in meetings, data gathering, and follow-up.

◆ **Trader:** Responsible for buying and selling securities.

◆ **Research analyst:** Performs research and analysis on investment options; provides information and makes recommendations to management on advisory-service products, investment selection, suitability guidelines, and reporting decisions.

◆ **Client-services administrator:** Initiates contact with clients to provide or obtain updated information, schedule meetings with preferred staff, and troubleshoot problems.

◆ **Customer support:** Answers incoming client calls regarding accounts, company and fund policies, practices, and services.

Administrative Functions

◆ **Office manager, office administrator, administrative assistant:** Responsible for overall general office operations, such as internal accounting, office equipment and supplies, benefits administration, and payroll coordination; may also coordinate the firm's website or other marketing tools. This is a catchall function in firms that do not employ individual staff members responsible for each (or some) of these functions.

◆ **Network administrator, information-systems manager:** Administers the firm's network; installs, configures, and maintains the firm's software and hardware; may provide computer support to staff.

◆ **Internal accountant, bookkeeper:** Responsible for internal accounting and generating the firm's financial statements.

◆ **Secretary, administrative assistant:** Performs secretarial and clerical duties such as typing correspondence, memoranda, reports, and meeting notes; schedules appointments and meetings; operates office equipment such as photocopier and fax machine.

◆ **Receptionist:** Greets and directs clients and other visitors; screens and routes telephone calls; may perform incidental typing or other routine clerical duties.

functions in addition to the ones defined here and must develop more detailed descriptions of each job, describing the specific role and responsibilities within the firm, as well as the performance expectations.

Defining Performance Expectations

Although certain individuals will likely perform more than one of the job functions described above, how will they know they're doing so successfully if the expectations of the jobs are not clear? The job descriptions should address these questions:

◆ What work experience, certification(s), degree(s), and tenure are required or desired?
◆ What is the primary function of individuals performing this job?
◆ How are they expected to spend their time in this job?
◆ To whom will they report?
◆ What is the technical skill set required to do this job well?
◆ What will be the process for evaluation?
◆ What are the criteria for measuring success?
  —Management responsibility for client relationships?
  —Revenue responsibility?
  —Business-development responsibility (internal, external, or both)?
  —Ability to complete work independently or with supervision?
  —Need to manage, supervise, or mentor others?
  —Volume or speed of work?
  —Number of hours worked?
◆ Are there nonquantitative criteria that will be part of the evaluation?

This detailed description will help clarify the hurdles that must be cleared and the performance standards that must be met in order for other candidates within or outside the organization to grow into the specific position. These performance expectations will also form the basis of the advancement guidelines and performance-based incentive plan.

The Nature of the Worker

Once the job is defined, you'll find it easier to identify the optimal characteristics required for individuals performing that work. With the proper framework in place, you're able to evaluate the right candidates for your business—whether from inside or outside the firm.

The cost of turnover is too high to take the selection and retention of people lightly. Financial advisers by nature are nurturers, so a greater focus on staff selection and development would not be out of place, especially when you consider the emotional and financial rewards of effective operating leverage. Identifying the right candidates is not as complex when you use the right approach.

Candidate Selection

One of our clients once said, "The biggest mistake we've ever made was hiring other people's debris." This was a blunt way of describing the raft of untalented people he had hired and subsequently fired. But what he discovered from this process was not that the people didn't have ability but rather that they didn't have the appropriate characteristics for the jobs they were hired to perform, even though they may have had a similar job at another firm. He discovered these employees were faking it in hopes of making it, but the nature of the work soon exposed their poor fit for the roles they were hired to fill. No amount of intelligence can overcome such weaknesses over time.

The single biggest reason for turnover in a financial-advisory practice is poor selection of candidates. We often find that individuals are mismatched to their jobs. They may be smart enough to fake it for the short term, but eventually they become burned out or bored, and their performance begins to suffer.

The most common reasons why financial advisers hire the wrong people are

♦ desperation
♦ reliance on the résumé
♦ friendship or personal relationship
♦ the job and criteria are not clearly defined

One client told us that when he inherited the responsibility for managing the staff, he felt as if he were directing "Theater of the Absurd." His predecessor had appointed a longtime employee to be responsible for hiring all other administrative staff. Over a three-year period, she had transformed the support team into a circus act. Each day was a new and interesting episode.

What the client soon discovered about this odd collection of staff was that they were all people who could be easily controlled by the person who had done the hiring. They weren't necessarily qualified for the job; nor did they have the potential to enhance the firm's culture. They were merely individuals who would not pose a threat to the long-time employee who was now their boss.

It is not uncommon in advisory firms to see similar examples of such hiring practices. Often a huge gulf exists between the capabilities of the practice owner and those of the staff so that the owner is not threatened or challenged. The downside of this approach is they often get people mismatched to the job or the culture they're trying to create, and the burden for the owner doesn't ease.

Although owners of advisory practices could employ the techniques used by more sophisticated organizations to hire the right people, they're often put off by the cost. But what is the cost of doing it wrong? Human resource experts say that replacing an employee costs a company somewhere between 150 percent and 200 percent of the person's salary in lost productivity, lost time in training, and a loss of momentum in the business.

Employers increase their odds of success with a new hire by employing the following techniques in the selection process:

♦ Interview
♦ Background check
♦ Psychometric and/or personality testing
♦ Ability testing
♦ Interest testing
♦ Job matching

By using these processes in evaluating candidates, you will get a good look at their past, present, and future. You see their past by reviewing their history—their résumé, education, and past employ-

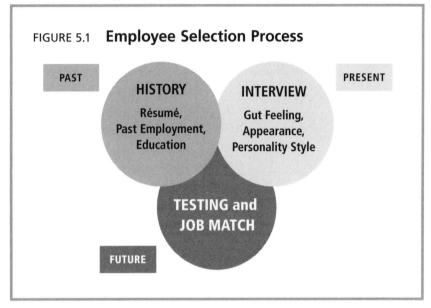

FIGURE 5.1   **Employee Selection Process**

Source: © Business Insight Technologies

ment. Through the interview process, you get a sense of their present—their professionalism, personality, and style, as well as your own
gut feeling about how they might fit into the organization. Through
job matching and testing for skills, abilities, motivations, interests,
and personality, you can also get a glimpse of the candidate's future
and the likelihood that the candidate will be a good fit for the job
and the organization (see *Figure 5.1*).

Unfortunately, most advisory firms end their evaluations after the
résumé and interview. Although a candidate's résumé may make it appear
that certain characteristics are present, that may not be the case. Indeed,
the résumé provides only part of the story. If you base your selection
on a résumé and an interview, you miss most of what's lurking under
the surface, which includes critical factors that will affect the candidate's
success in the position (see *Figure 5.2*). To get below the surface, you
need to broaden your evaluation process to include background checks
and psychometric testing, which will help you evaluate ability, motivation, and interests. These are both legitimate and legal tools in hiring
people, providing you don't abuse them or use them in a discriminat-
ing manner. The success rate of hires increases substantially as these
tools are employed in a meaningful way (see *Figure 5.3*).

FIGURE 5.2 **What's Lurking Underneath?**

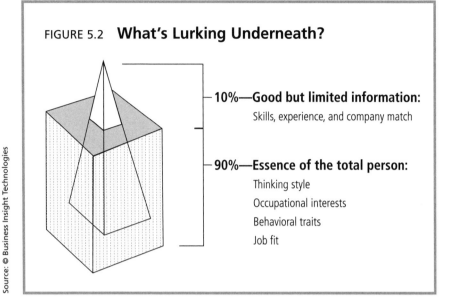

10%—Good but limited information:
Skills, experience, and company match

90%—Essence of the total person:
Thinking style
Occupational interests
Behavioral traits
Job fit

Source: © Business Insight Technologies

FIGURE 5.3 **Use All Resources to Ensure Success**

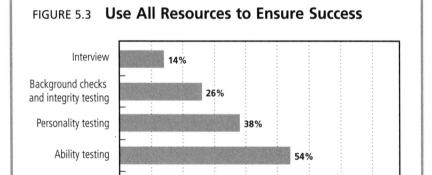

Source: © Business Insight Technologies

Job Benchmarking

Most advisers recognize the value of benchmarking in the context of investment performance. The same technique is applicable to hiring individuals, although benchmarking in this context is slightly different. Once the job is defined, the employer (often with the help of an outside expert) can design a benchmark for the position. To design the benchmark, it's important first to identify the characteristics of an individual for that role—for example, personality, motivation, and interest. In an ideal world, to create the optimal profile, you would also identify how other successful employees compared with that benchmark. Larger firms have such a database to draw from, which is why we encourage testing of existing staff. Such data also serve as a tool for more effective management of those individuals.

The benchmark you create for the position allows you to match the person to the job. Do you want someone who is good with numbers, with data, with concepts? For example, what would be the optimal attributes of a portfolio manager in terms of the ability for working with numbers, with concepts, with data, or with people? Should the candidate be process oriented or event oriented? Of course, you want someone who excels in all areas, but the reality is that each of us has a unique combination of strengths, so we're not ideally suited for every job.

Certain individuals can perform extraordinarily well in areas outside of their natural abilities for short periods, but they will experience serious burnout before their career is over. For example, if a new hire has no natural orientation for dealing with people, yet she's hired to develop new business, she'll eventually find excuses for not initiating contact with prospects and sources of referral. Or if an employee doesn't have a natural bent for working with numbers but he's put into an analytical position, his work will eventually become sloppy and filled with errors. This isn't a work ethic issue and it doesn't mean they don't have the intelligence to perform these functions. It means they don't have the interest and personality that's right for the job.

When you benchmark the position, you can test candidates for their suitability to perform the work. This allows you to see beyond the candidate's education or experience and evaluate their natural aptitude to perform the tasks (see *Figure 5.4*).

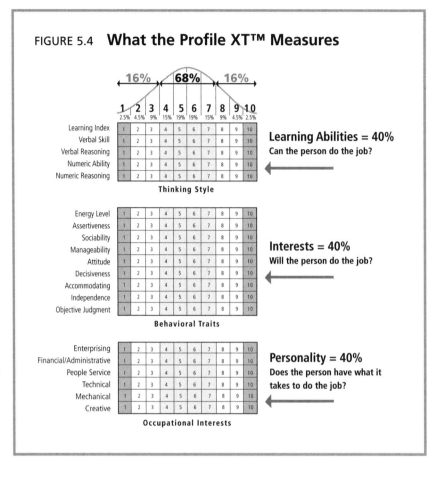

FIGURE 5.4 **What the Profile XT™ Measures**

Source: © Business Insight Technologies

If you've ever heard yourself saying something like, "The problem is that this generation just doesn't see work the way I do," then you have become your parent—or your first boss. Every generation going back to the beginning of time believes that it works harder, acts smarter, and behaves more honestly than the one that follows. While it may be true that people today value life balance over workaholism, that's not a bad thing. Unreasonable expectations and poor job matching are the bad things.

Certainly it's not uncommon to find individuals who have extraordinary ability and the capacity to learn quickly and perform well in a job. But you'll also find that many of those individuals will lose their enthusiasm for the job quickly as it becomes mundane, uninteresting, or unsuited to their work style. By knowing their orientation, you can place them in the right position within your firm—whether it's a client-service, analytical, compliance, management, or sales position or some other role that you deem critical.

Professional Development

S TAFF DEVELOPMENT BEGINS with the definition of performance
expectations for the specific position, as discussed in chapter 5.
The discussion then must go beyond the specific measurables for the
job and articulate the behaviors and values employees must demonstrate. That's done by defining what's important to the organization. At Moss Adams, for example, we've adopted a concept called
PILLAR, which guides all of our hiring, staff development, coaching, and advancement. PILLAR stands for

P —passion for excellence
I —integrity
L —lifetime learning
L —lead by example
A—a balanced life
R—respect for others

The concept encourages both professional and personal development, and we find these characteristics form the building blocks
for a dynamic organization. To create a culture that embraces this
concept, each element must be incorporated into the performance-
review process and into how we go about selecting new partners or
shareholders for the firm. Your firm's values statement should be sim-
ilarly integrated into your approach to developing human capital.

In a service business, all members of the professional staff must
focus on both bringing in new clients and serving them well. But as
you can see from the PILLAR framework, you can apply a standard

of evaluation that goes beyond revenue production. To help evaluate how well individuals adopt PILLAR as a tenet of their professional life within our firm, we use an appraisal process.

The Appraisal Process

Employees need and want feedback. Whether he's the boss or the lowest-ranking employee, a person wants and needs to know how others think he's doing.

What to Evaluate

By employing the discipline of a formal appraisal process, you can evaluate an individual's specific performance goals for the appraisal period. You can also explore issues important to your culture and use what you learn as a foundation for coaching people to achieve higher levels of performance. The numbers can be measured on their own. The challenge for you is to evaluate all of the other elements that combine to make your culture what it is—or what you want it to be.

For example, to evaluate passion for excellence, you might rate your staff in terms of the extent to which they

- ♦ demonstrate pride in their work
- ♦ complete their work on time and on budget
- ♦ solve problems effectively
- ♦ meet client-service expectations
- ♦ communicate clearly and listen well

To measure integrity, you might rate the staff on whether they
- ♦ behave unethically or tolerate unethical behavior of others
- ♦ maintain their continuing-education requirements willingly
- ♦ put the firm at risk with their own behavior

To assess lifetime learning, you might explore whether they
- ♦ are committed to expanding their knowledge and education
- ♦ apply technology tools well

To find out whether they lead by example, you might ask whether they

♦ demonstrate a positive attitude toward the firm's goals
♦ take responsibility for actions and accept responsibility for mistakes
♦ act as a role model or mentor for others

To measure a balanced life, you'll want to observe how well they

♦ act as a role model in how they balance business and personal activities
♦ avoid becoming obsessive about work
♦ avoid becoming obsessive about play. (Remember, a balanced life doesn't mean taking a lot of days off from work but rather keeping work and nonwork in sync.)

To assess their respect for others, you may want to rate them on whether they

♦ respond to feedback from others respectfully
♦ keep you informed of progress on client work, if appropriate
♦ treat colleagues and subordinates respectfully
♦ respect clients in what they say and do and how they respond to issues

Your challenge is to make sure that every person in the organization adopts not just one of the virtues but rather the total concept. Partners, for example, will say that PILLAR is not appropriate for them because nobody would expect them to lead "a balanced life." After all, they're the most important person on the planet and God only knows what would happen if they didn't spend all their time in the office. But it's particularly critical that partners, of all people, exhibit the values and behavior that have been defined as important to the organization.

We must continually remind our partners at Moss Adams that their succession (and, consequently, retirement plan) depends on the admittance of future partners. And if people think that partnership is a dog's life, they won't aspire to it. This doesn't apply only to the balanced-life concept but to the other virtues as well, like passion for excellence and lifelong learning. We expect all of our people—but especially our partners—to lead by example. Behavioral change, unfortunately, comes slowly—unless it comes by virtue of a near-death experience.

We try to weed out those in the firm who cannot embrace these concepts. No matter how big their economic contribution to the firm, people who set negative examples eventually sap the firm of its lifeblood. The long-term economic toll of bad apples is significant.

PILLAR, of course, is just an example of how one firm reinforces its expectations and the culture it's trying to create. Each firm must establish its own boundaries and expectations, although your firm is free to borrow the PILLAR approach if you feel it applies. The key is to be clear about what you expect of everyone, know what culture you want to build and sustain, and have a means for evaluating and reinforcing the right behavior. Should you choose to ignore all of the soft issues and focus solely on making money, that is a clear statement of culture and will appeal to some people. But we would recommend broadening your perspective.

How to Evaluate

Most firms that are successful in reinforcing behavior do so through a structured evaluation process in which peers evaluate peers, supervisors evaluate subordinates, and subordinates evaluate supervisors (upstream evaluation).

A peer evaluation allows your colleagues to judge you and your performance against your performance objectives and the culture that you're trying to create. By pointing out when you're drifting away from the mark or calling attention to your strengths or weaknesses, they give you the opportunity and the insight to improve.

An upstream evaluation allows your subordinates to evaluate you objectively, knowing there will be no negative consequences from showing you how those who work for you perceive you. This is critical for building a dynamic organization because if you're not trusted, respected, or liked, you will lose your ability to leverage your business effectively.

Of course, the smaller the firm, the harder it is to employ these tools effectively because everyone knows the source of the comments. That's why you must encourage openness and candor when eliciting these appraisals and make it clear that you will not seek retribution for criticism. As you listen to the constructive comments and you work to change either the perception or the reality, you begin to create a team atmosphere of trust and respect that contributes to the success of the business.

Larger practices can create a more structured appraisal process and, to some degree, preserve anonymity for subordinates who are doing upstream evaluations of the practice leaders. Some firms outsource this process to consultants to ensure objectivity and trust in the process. If the owner has a business coach, for example, the coach would be an appropriate choice for compiling the responses, and the coach would gain a better foundation for coaching the individual in business matters.

In the late 1990s, we were asked by a prominent financial adviser to serve in this intermediary role. He seemed to be a living example of someone "lonely at the top." It wounded him when he heard criticism of himself from people in the firm or even from others in the industry. Yet he was not sure how to minimize this or even what issues to address. To help, we created an upstream evaluation process that applied not only to him but also to anyone in the firm who had employees reporting to them. Over a three-year period, we tracked and monitored each manager's evaluations, but especially his, since he was most eager for the feedback.

In the first year, the semiannual evaluations were very tentative; the staff would give him very high scores (on a scale of one to five), but their comments tended to be more critical and out of sync with the numeric evaluation they assigned. We used the comments as the basis for counseling him. In the second year, when the staff saw that the owner did not blast them for what they said, they tended to score more accurately and their comments were more substantive. By the third year, we saw a perceptible increase in trust.

Although we were pleased to see the evaluation process take root, we were even more pleased to see how constructive feedback on issues of importance to the firm helped the owner and his senior-level people improve their performance and their relationship with their team *and* reduce turnover. With each evaluation, we were able to counsel the owner on how well he communicated with the staff, how well he recognized their contributions to the firm, how he awarded promotions, and how effectively he encouraged employees to improve their own performance. Over time, the business became both more efficient and more profitable. But oddly enough, this improvement did not result from a greater emphasis on sales; it occurred because there was greater emphasis on the firm's mission and culture and a unified commitment to the firm's goals.

Coaching and Development

We find that the biggest mistake advisers make is hiring people who do not match the job. The second biggest mistake is failing to coach and develop people once they have them in the fold. One of the most glaring gaps in the human-capital capabilities of advisers is their lack of ability or interest in training, coaching, developing, and mentoring others in their organization.

Once you have defined the expectations of the job—both specific performance criteria and cultural values—and evaluated employees against those criteria via the appraisal process, you need to take what you learned and coach employees to higher levels of performance. In some cases, you need to evaluate whether they are, in fact, coachable or trainable. Will they be able to make a contribution in the roles you've assigned them? Do they have the ability, motivation, and interest to perform in those roles? Human-capital management is an ongoing process of recruiting, evaluating, and re-recruiting.

Figure 6.1 illustrates the coaching concept, depicting the balance between skill and job fit. As shown in the illustration, employees with a high skill level and high job fit are the ones that need to be retained, protected, and coached to even higher performance and more opportunity. Those with a low skill level and low job fit must be coached out of the organization. In situations where the skill level is high but the job fit is low, you may consider finding a better fit for the individual within the organization. Further training is indicated when the job fit is high and the skill level is low.

In addition to the feedback process, you'll want to consider aligning your strategy with your continuing-education program for your

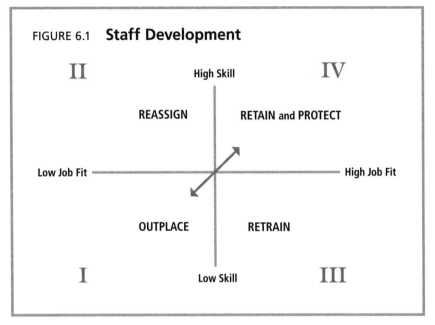

FIGURE 6.1   **Staff Development**

Source: © Moss Adams LLP

staff. One of the main reasons people give for leaving firms is that the work was not challenging enough. There are any number of reasons for this; possibly your client base has simple needs. But more likely, the practice leader is reluctant to delegate challenging work because he or she lacks confidence in the staff person's ability to perform. Define the training and education required to build that person's skills and your own confidence, then assign him or her work that's up to the new standard. This method of continual improvement is critical to practice success.

In Ayn Rand's classic *Atlas Shrugged* (Dutton Books, 1992), the character Dagney Taggert, in her search for meaning, talks to a group of businessmen who had retreated from an unwelcoming world to form their own community called Galt's Gulch. They tell Taggert, "It is not your obedience we seek, but your conviction." This is a good principle by which to run your business. If your people do not have a passion for your business, then none of you will be fulfilled. This passion will come, first, from selecting your team well and matching them to the right jobs and, second, from creating the type of workplace that will allow them to flourish.

The Workplace

Once the nature and scope of the work has been clearly defined and the right workers are in the right jobs, the challenge is to create a workplace where motivated people can flourish. A place where

♦ employees are satisfied and motivated
♦ the culture is one of respect, trust, and caring
♦ personal and business growth are aligned
♦ achievement and challenge are the standard
♦ performance is recognized

What Really Drives Retention?

When we surveyed the staff of financial-advisory practices about their attitudes and experiences, we found that the No. 1 reason employees were looking for work elsewhere was that they lacked confidence in management. "How could this be?" the blind-sided owner might ask. "How could those nonproductive people have the cheek to question management? Why, they should be happy they have a job!"

If you've ever found yourself looking at your staff as an expense to be managed, rather than an asset on which you produce a return, you're likely creating an environment in which individuals lose their motivation. The observation that money is not what keeps people happy has become an adage. Obviously, when you play around with people's compensation, it has an impact. But we've found that if an employee's compensation is within 10 percent of the market norm, individuals won't leave your firm unless there are other factors that make the work environment unpleasant, unchallenging, or unsuccessful.

Oddly enough, most advisers tell us that the key to their success is the "family environment" they believe they foster in their firms. This is mostly true in the industry, if you hold that most families are dysfunctional. When other factors come into play, the culture of closeness does not hold up. The family concept is a convenient term when the owner of the practice is able to share some of his or her wealth because of a good year or a big new client. Naturally, people are happy when you give them money. But as one adviser put it, "A hooker will never love you." In other words, if you're using money to bond with the staff, you're not building the culture you hope to achieve. When you rely on a culture of closeness, you're often forced to avoid hard discussions with members of the staff who are not fulfilling your expectations or meeting up to their own abilities. Many financial advisers prefer to avoid conflict, and the pain they experience personally in having to confront a problem is almost paralyzing.

Alfie Kohn wrote a great book on this subject called *Punished by Rewards: The Trouble With Gold Stars, Incentive Plans, A's, Praise, and Other Bribes* (Mariner Books, 1999). His premise is that business owners are often like busy parents: rather than using active management as the means for imbuing the "family" with the values and ethic they deem important, they try to create behavior change by throwing money at them. Imagine a small child, he explains, who cries and wails and screams. To quiet him, a parent gives him candy. Even a young child understands cause and effect. What has he now learned to do if he wants more candy?

As the owner and manager, it's your job to create a working environment in which motivated people can flourish. Critical to such an approach is proper job matching, so that you have the best chance of leveraging off your staff's abilities, interest, and motivation. But aside from placing people in the right jobs, it's also important that you create a challenging, dynamic environment in which individuals have the opportunity to grow.

In one study of staffing and compensation issues within financial-advisory firms, we asked the employees of these firms what issues were on their minds. The survey revealed some very compelling and disturbing perceptions of their workplace, which validated what we had been hearing from other staffers in our individual consulting projects. Almost a quarter of them said they were currently looking for another job. Asked why they were considering leaving, they responded: to pursue better opportunities elsewhere or, in many cases, to leave the profession entirely. So not only did their bosses undermine their motivation to continue working for the firm, they soured their appetite for working in the industry at all. It seems the dissatisfaction had mainly to do with lack of challenging work, lack of confidence in management, and lack of recognition. All of these problems are fixable. Only a small percentage said that low compensation was a factor in their deciding to leave, though the typical adviser believes money is the only reason people leave their firm.

When you consider that the primary reasons to hire staff in the first place is to create better leverage and delegate the work you're not particularly skilled at or interested in, then employee perceptions about lack of challenge are especially jarring. Firms that have high retention rates among valued employees do several things well:

♦ They have a management team that is aligned and cohesive and has a shared focus.
♦ They have the right people in the right jobs.
♦ They maximize leadership strengths and focus resources on strategic priorities.
♦ They have an organizational structure that's efficient, productive, and leverageable, while enhancing growth and supporting current business operations.
♦ They link business goals to position responsibilities, performance metrics, and reward systems.
♦ They emphasize teamwork, accountability, and commonality.
♦ They attract, retain, develop, and reward talents.
♦ They celebrate successes.

Managing Culture

Organizational culture is one of those soft and squishy concepts that make financial-advisers-turned-business-managers queasy. It's also one of the primary drivers of staff satisfaction and staff turnover. It boils down to answering the question, "What's it like to work here?" When it's working well, the culture is the key element that holds the organization together, gives everyone a common identity, and drives commitment and behavior.

The keys to managing culture are:

♦ Knowing what the current culture is—getting feedback
♦ Knowing what the future culture should be
♦ Clearly defining and communicating both
♦ Being prepared to commit to a lengthy process of change
♦ Tying all factors and functions together
♦ Continually monitoring
♦ Ensuring that change is valued

Managing Difficult People

The downside of growing your business is that you have more people to manage. Some financial advisers are predisposed to this role and are able to follow their instincts; others are not. But we do not know of a single business owner who hasn't struggled with the question, "Am I managing difficult people, or do I have difficulty managing people?"

One of the challenges for advisers is the idea that everyone they employ is a friend or a member of the family. As a consequence, the practice drifts and the owner suffers in silence. We know of multiple situations in which the firm has made a modest profit for years, and the owner has taken out no salary or no more than a meager draw for many months. In many of these situations, the staff is paid more than the owner.

Why does this occur? The most common refrains we hear from the owners are, "No one is accountable here!" and "There are no consequences if they don't perform." That's when we grab the owners by the lapel, shake them hard, look them in the eye, and tell them, "You're the boss! *You* hold your staff accountable." And if your so-called friends—the people in your organization whom you cannot confront—fail to fulfill what is expected of them, then they obviously don't regard this friendship as highly as you do. Oddly enough, the same people are likely to be annoyed with you because you're not setting boundaries and holding them accountable.

An article in a parenting magazine not long ago noted how each successive generation of parents has become more permissive in rearing its children. It observed that our contemporaries—especially those raised in more authoritarian households—desire to be friends first, parents second. They proudly boast about this warm and fuzzy quality that had been absent in their own childhood even as they whined about how incorrigible their kids have become. Many advisers apply this same theory to managing and leading their staff. In an ideal world, you would have created a workplace in which motivated people can manage themselves, but the reality is that most employees need some structure, focus, and reinforcement at least some of the time.

Of course, advisers often want to keep their business small to avoid bureaucracy. But many think this means they can also avoid conflict with their staff. That's not possible. Having structure doesn't mean you can't have a happy, fun, cheerful, and even loose environment. It does mean that an absence of processes, protocols, measurements, and evaluations will lead to dysfunction.

If you have ever worked for somebody else, you should ask yourself the question, "Have I ever been mismanaged?" There's a high probability your answer will be yes. Somewhere in your career, you've probably worked for someone who did not appreciate you, respect you, or pay you appropriately. Assuming your perception about that experience is correct, have you ever thought about how you lead your own people and do you apply the management lessons you learned from that personal experience? Like parents, we often apply approaches we were conditioned to learn, which causes those we're supervising to rebel.

It can also be useful—as you recall what it was like to work for someone else—to reflect on the conversations you had with coworkers. Think about the after-work pub crawls, where your antipathy toward your employer grew increasingly passionate in proportion to the pints consumed. Or how about the times you challenged your bosses and threatened to quit? In hindsight, how much of your complaint was valid, and how much of your rage was a result of your own insecurity? That's not to say your frustration was unjustified, but immaturity may have pushed your reaction out of proportion, and your attitude may have portrayed you as "not a team player."

The recognition of what's troubling your staff and how you're relating to them may help you to deal with those employees you regard as "difficult." But before you decide this is just another out-of-touch consultant who blames the parent or the boss, it's not impossible that you may indeed have a jerk or two working for you, and there may be nothing you can do about them except to kick them out.

In our consulting with financial-services firms on organizational, staffing, and strategic issues, we must delve into the human dynamics of the business. We find some common reasons for discontent that can usually be solved by getting the strategy and the structure back into alignment and by helping the businesses to improve internal communication. In many other cases, we find that clearly defining a career path goes a long way toward getting people to focus on a goal instead of on their navel. Nevertheless, there may very well be an employee or a partner who single-handedly sucks the energy and enthusiasm right out of the practice. Such people are not happy unless they're unhappy. They're carriers of a potentially virulent disease we call "staff rot."

Taking Action

Your obligation as a manager is to assess whether the person is a chronic problem or whether the attitude is justified and fixable. It's difficult to differentiate between the two, although it's often worth the effort. People who challenge you can often be intelligent, driven, and dynamic individuals whose energy and creativity you'd do well to harness to help propel your business forward. In many cases, they can be tremendous revenue producers, so the dollars blind our judgment.

But if advisers were to look back at their biggest management mistakes, they would probably admit that they did not deal with these types of people quickly enough. And by people, we mean both partners and staff. Such individuals have the uncanny ability to make you feel like their problems are your fault. Our tendency is to show them love, accommodate them, acknowledge their pain, and throw money at them in the hope that we can be redeemed in their eyes. But appeasement does not usually work for the long term when you're dealing with people who are immature and insecure. What ails them is a moving target. The problem is especially unsolvable if they cannot tell you specifically what it would reasonably take for them to feel fulfilled in your business. But at what point does it become necessary to confront them? If they suffer in silence, or triangulate the complaint by venting to people other than you, your situation is close to hopeless, so it's time to act.

It's estimated—in *The War for Talent* (Harvard Business School Press, 2001)—that about 15 percent of the workforce within any company is nonperforming (not meeting critical success initiatives). Imagine what you could do with 15 percent of the payroll. The chance to add 15 percent to the bottom line and reinvest or redirect it to top performers is certainly worth your attention.

We have helped many firms to reconfigure their human-capital equation through the strategy of the five Bs: buy, build, borrow, bounce, and bind. We use a series of tools such as Profile™ or Kolbe™ benchmarking, interviewing, organizational surveying and auditing, and plan redesign to help our clients reconfigure their human capital to maximize results and profits. There are several steps you can take now.

First, if you do not have a formal evaluation process, you must implement one, as described earlier in this chapter. Formal appraisals give you a foundation for counseling the staff member.

There is a practical model for resolving differences among people and helping steer behavior either to exceptional performance or out the door. We call that process the DESCO model, and it works best when the following five steps are deployed:

1. Describe the specific observed behavior that you want to discuss.
2. Express your feelings, reactions, and concerns about the behavior.
3. Suggest an alternative behavior or set of behaviors.
4. Consequences (state them).
5. Offer support to help the person "move up or move out."

Second, you must listen and respond to the employee, not react. If the employee's point is valid, you should obviously acknowledge it and deal with it. If you don't feel you can be responsive to the complaint, then you must be forthright about the reason why. If the problem is a perpetual thorn in the employee's paw, then explore whether there is another solution. If it's a nuisance issue, you can deal with it. But if the problem is too great for either of you to overcome and it's affecting morale, then encourage the employee to seek work elsewhere. But be sure you understand whether he or she is the problem or you are.

One employee of an advisory firm, for example, felt that the owner had encouraged him to do something unethical. This event had occurred a couple of years earlier, and it was difficult to confirm whether it occurred the way the employee recalled it—the communication between the two was loose and subject to interpretation.

But no such request was ever made again by the owner. Nonetheless, for the next two years, whenever there was conflict or this employee became overwhelmed with work, he would bring up the issue, always concluding with, "And this is why I'm not sure I can keep working here." Situations like this become a distraction and manipulative. Whether or not the complaint is valid, if such an affront could not be buried after two years, it's unlikely it will ever be resolved. Yet the issue defined the relationship between employee and employer and caused the boss to look for ways to appease this person through money, extra attention, time off, a new title, and so on. Obviously, this employee had found the right button to push, and the boss's reactions encouraged him to continue with this strategy of torment and guilt.

Third, consider using the psychometric tests described previously, such as Profile™ or Kolbe™, to determine whether the individual is truly suitable for the job. We always encourage such assessments be applied in the hiring process because they provide tremendous insight into whether individuals have the motivation, personality, interests, and ability to perform certain work. We also find them to be a powerful means of understanding what makes people tick. Bad behavior can be triggered by boredom or frustration. For example, your employee may have been hired for a highly technical position and was judged qualified by his experiences, background, and education. But if his mind map indicates that he cannot sustain a long-term interest in such detailed or complex work, then he'll burn out like a supernova. He himself may recognize he's no longer able to fulfill your expectations. Rather than owning up to this, he will lash out at you as the reason he's foundering.

As with parenting, there isn't much practical training available for bosses until they're on the job and in the line of fire. But good advisers tend to be intuitive people, so applying these techniques to the staff may help you get to the root cause of the issue. That said, do not overindulge those who will not conform to the culture you're trying to build. Ultimately, it's up to employees to act their age. If they're unable to respond positively to constructive solutions that are within the framework of your business purpose and expectations, it may be best to cut your losses and find people who will. As Winston Churchill said, "Graveyards are filled with indispensable people."

Hiring Your Boss: Do You Need a CEO?

Does your advisory practice need a chief executive officer? As the financial-advisory profession evolves from offering well-paying jobs to providing real career paths, more and more growing practices are concluding that they do. In the *2003 Compensation and Staffing Survey* conducted by Moss Adams for the Financial Planning Association, we found that 52 percent of firms that generate more than $1 million in annual revenues employ the services of a CEO. Clearly, every growing business needs a leader who will provide strategy and planning and who has executive management skills to translate that vision into action—whether or not that person is a professional CEO.

Unfortunately, most financial advisers have little or no training or background in business management, so they're forced to hire from the outside. But practitioners who do hire a CEO are often disappointed with their hiring decisions. It's difficult for most owners of advisory firms to give up the strategic leadership role in their business. That's why firms rarely succeed when they hire a full-time CEO who has no role in client service or development. It's virtually impossible emotionally for advisers to surrender the responsibilities of leading the firm.

However, professional management is important whether it's the responsibility of the owners themselves or of outside hires. Depending on the size of the firm, the position could be a general manager or a chief operating officer (COO). As chairman and CEO of the practice, the individual reports to the owner, who most likely is the founder or one of the lead advisers. The general manager's role is to be accountable for implementation of financial management, operations, information technology, and human-capital strategies within the firm. Occasionally, depending on the size of the firm, he or she may also be responsible for sales and marketing. The key concept is that the manager makes sure the infrastructure of the firm is operating efficiently, effectively, and productively.

So why do so many advisers who hire CEOs end up disappointed? In consulting with many such firms about their organization and compensation plans after they've become disillusioned with the experience, we've discovered some common complaints about the CEOs they've hired:

♦ It costs too much for management; I could do what he (she) does.
♦ We're paying too much for what we get.
♦ She's trying to create a strategy that I'm not comfortable with.
♦ He's making decisions unilaterally.
♦ She will not handle details.
♦ He will not address the big strategic questions.
♦ She has poor people skills.
♦ We cannot get the reports we want and need.
♦ He has no sense of urgency or priority.
♦ Her answer for everything is to hire more staff.
♦ He cannot deal with conflict or difficult situations.
♦ She wants to renegotiate her contract.
♦ He says we are not clear in what we want from him.

Common Mistakes in Hiring a CEO

Although some of these observations are likely true, the core of the problem is a hiring issue. Too often, the person hired for this role was chosen based on the impressiveness of the résumé and (especially) big-company experience rather than on any specific qualifications to run a small, financial-services business. And often the cost of hiring such a person is out of proportion to the size and complexity of the business, which puts added strain on the relationship. More often than not, the owners of the practice cannot comfortably delegate the responsibilities they should to a CEO, who is responsible for bringing the business to the next level. Is it any wonder that these CEOs do not fulfill the expectations of the owners who hired them?

What follows are the most common mistakes we see advisers make in hiring professional management.

Failure to clearly define the roles and expectations of the individual CEO. Most financial-advisory practices are small businesses—certainly too small to be consumed by titles and size of offices. Yet the common misperception is that a firm needs to have a bona fide CEO at the helm before it can be regarded as a business. In their book *Navigating Change: How CEOs, Top Teams, and Boards Steer Transformation* (Harvard Business School Press, 1998), Donald Hambrick, David Nadler, and Michael Tushman suggest that the role of a CEO falls into three broad categories:

1. *Envisioning.* Successful CEOs share an ability to articulate and communicate a vision of the organization that captures the imagination of the people they lead.

2. *Energizing.* Effective CEOs energize their people by continually and publicly demonstrating their own sense of personal excitement and total engagement. They consistently convey a sense of absolute confidence in the organization's ability to achieve the most challenging goals.

3. *Enabling.* Effective CEOs find realistic ways to give people the confidence, authority, and resources they need to work toward their shared objectives.

If you examine these roles, you begin to realize that either these are the functions you personally are supposed to perform as the leader of the business, or you have to have the self-confidence to vest your new leader with this authority. More important, you have to decide if what you're looking for is truly a CEO or just a general manager to perform the management and personnel tasks that you would rather not do.

Failure to link the hiring of a CEO to a business strategy. Every practice-management decision should be tied into your business strategy. For example, if your vision is to grow your practice to three times its current size in the next five years, you'll want to recruit leaders who have experience with rapidly growing businesses. On the other hand, if you want to build a dominant regional firm, you might do better with someone well versed in your local market or skilled at acquiring and consolidating smaller independent businesses. Furthermore, you want to reward those leaders for helping you achieve certain benchmarks in your growth. If you do not have clarity of vision, you may as well be operating in the dark. The consequence will be multiple false starts and thousands of wasted dollars.

Many hires within financial-advisory practices occur because the owner stumbles on somebody who has become available. This mistake happens with all positions. Rather than thinking about what the organization should look like to better achieve its goals, owners react to perceived opportunities because the résumé is so impressive. Indeed, advisers often exhibit a bias toward hiring based on seductive résumés touting advanced degrees and big-company experience. The process should be more deliberate:

♦ What are the responsibilities that I want to delegate?
♦ Where are the leadership gaps that are impeding the firm's progress?
♦ What level of revenue must I generate to support this position?
♦ How will I know I've hired the right person, or how will I know if I've hired the wrong person?
♦ What characteristics must the person have to improve my practice?
♦ What job experiences or education does the candidate need for this role?

With this framework, practitioners can be more thoughtful about the position they're trying to fill and what their expectations are.

Failure to interview properly. It's essential to probe for real insight into an individual's makeup, aptitude, motivation, interests, and personality. Literally hundreds of psychometric tools are available that serve as useful sources of insight and information into how individuals are likely to perform their jobs.

It's not as important to hire the most intelligent people as it is to hire folks who have an aptitude or ability to quickly learn in the areas in which you want them to be strong. In particular, you need to evaluate their general abilities as well as their ability to work with numbers, words, or concepts. One of these may be more

important than the others. It's important to evaluate what motivates them—people, data, or things. In other words, do they tend
to be more social or more attached to their computers? Are they
hands on or hands off?

It's important to evaluate personality to ensure the candidate fits
your benchmark for the position and is compatible with the culture
you're trying to create. Some critical criteria include:

♦ *Self-reliance.* Is she a collaborator or independent? Submissive
  or assertive?
♦ *Process orientation.* Is he innovative or orderly and predictable?
  Reactive or organized?
♦ *Work style.* Is she analytical and self-sufficient or group-oriented
  and outgoing?
♦ *Social skills.* Can he take criticism or does he overreact? Does he
  have passion or is he a dullard? Is he frank?

Most leadership positions require a blending of these attributes.
But before hiring, you should establish a benchmark of the optimal
characteristics for that specific job, a blend that will suit the job, suit
you, and suit your organization.

**Failure to establish measurable criteria for evaluating perfor-
mance and to tie compensation to expectations.** Being clear about
what you expect your CEO to accomplish is vital both to the hiring process and to your ongoing management efforts. If you do not
know specifically what you want someone to do, how can you know
if you've found the right person? Sure, part of a CEO's job typically
is to help devise a strategy for your business and then to build the
team to implement it. Those are specific tasks that require specific
skills. But as the owner, you can't delegate all strategic planning to
a CEO; you need to have a clear vision of where you want the business to go.

At this point, your challenge is to decide whether you should
serve in the management role, the leadership role, or both. Between
your vision for the practice and its fruition lies a long shadow: a
shadow of doubt, of ability, of time. If your time is better spent on
client service or on business development, then try not to let your

ego get in the way of effective management. If the role is not for you, come clean and focus your talents where you can make the greatest impact on your business. But if you engage professional management or delegate these duties to others within your firm, you may need to work on keeping your reactions in check. If you hired well and were clear about your expectations, you'll be far better off allowing your managers to do their jobs than to insinuate yourself into the minutiae of their decisions.

Compensation Planning

ADVISORY FIRMS SPEND more money on professional and staff compensation than on any other expense. In fact, if these firms defined compensation appropriately, it would be clear that they actually invest more money in compensation than in any other area of the business. The challenge for advisers is to think of compensation as an investment, consider how they choose to allocate that investment, and determine what kind of return they expect on that investment.

Developed deliberately, a compensation plan can be a recruiting tool, a retention tool, a behavior driver, and, most important, a communication tool for expressing what's important to the organization. A compensation plan defines the behavior the firm values and will pay for—and the behavior it values so much that it will pay extra for it.

The mistakes advisory firms make in designing their compensation plans are remarkably consistent:

♦ They pay as if they're rewarding production, when they're trying to create a firm culture.

♦ There is no consensus among the partners on the underlying compensation philosophy—what they believe and what they want to accomplish with their plan.

♦ They develop the compensation plan in a void, with no strategic context.

♦ They don't relate compensation to performance goals or to a performance appraisal process.

♦ They focus too much on the total dollars to be paid—the *what*— and not enough on how that compensation will be structured— the *how*—and what they're trying to accomplish—the *why*.

Many conversations we have with advisers who believe they're struggling with compensation issues begin with a question like "I hired a new guy—just couldn't pass him up. How much should I pay him?" Even more begin with questions like "Our turnover has been really high, especially among young advisers. We must have a compensation problem. Can you help us address it?" Both of these questions, of course, point to issues larger than just compensation—issues typically related to strategy, culture, and career path. Compensation, however, is often perceived as the easiest problem to address, or the easiest way to address a problem, even if the problem is not actually related to compensation.

The best firms in the industry have a formal compensation process —a deliberate way in which they structure people's pay—and they have a clear understanding of where compensation fits into their larger human-capital plan. Most advisers are tempted to begin their human-capital plan with compensation. However, it's truly impossible to design effective compensation until you've envisioned the organization you're investing in and the desired performance you're paying for. The most critical steps and conversations in developing a compensation plan arise before the issue of compensation is ever addressed. A meaningful compensation plan typically arises at the *end* of a process that looks like this:

1. Develop the business strategy.
2. Define the roles, responsibilities, and staffing model.
3. Define the desired behaviors and performance expectations.
4. Hire the right people.
5. Design a compensation plan to reinforce the desired behaviors.

Developing a Plan

There are four absolute truths about an effective compensation plan within a financial-advisory firm:

♦ It must be aligned with your strategy.

♦ It must reinforce the behavior you desire.
♦ It must be affordable to the business.
♦ It must be in harmony with the expectations of your staff.

Strategic Alignment

In financial-advisory firms, the most common example of misalign-ment relates to both client selection and product or service offering. We once consulted with a firm that had a stated commitment to build its business around high-net-worth individuals. However, the firm's incentive program was tied to the number of new clients each adviser obtained, regardless of the client's profile. It happened that one adviser had a pipeline into a plan administration firm that referred him large volumes of 401(k) plan assets to manage. You might argue that assets are assets, but obviously the approach to servicing 401(k) participants is a whole lot different from the approach needed for wealthy indi-viduals, and the margins are usually not as large. The firm had built up its estate- and charitable-planning capability to be responsive to the complex needs of wealthy individuals, but the people filling these functions were idle because of the nature of the clients that were actu-ally being brought in. In this example, and in many advisory firms, the incentive plan in place was reinforcing behavior contrary to the firm's stated strategy. The very process of defining a business strat-egy implies focus. The incentive plan supporting a business's strategy must be likewise focused on the *right* behavior.

Compensation philosophy statement. One way to ensure the alignment of an advisory firm's pay practices with its business strategy is by articulating a compensation philosophy. As an example, Kochis Fitz, a large San Francisco–based advisory firm has a compensation philosophy statement describing the corporate and cultural values important to the company's future success. This compensation philosophy statement ensures an alignment between the firm's strategic direction and compensation strategy (see "Compensation Philosophy at Kochis Fitz").

Given this compensation philosophy, it's relatively easy, even as an outsider, to imagine the kinds of compensation decisions this under-lying philosophy might drive and the kinds of compensation pro-grams that would contradict or undermine this philosophy. Often,

Compensation Philosophy at Kochis Fitz

THE COMPENSATION PROGRAM at Kochis Fitz is guided by the following principles:

1. Team performance should be emphasized over individual performance.
2. Incentives should work to build and support a team approach and a team environment.
3. Compensation should be externally competitive and internally equitable.
4. The compensation strategy should be aligned with the business strategy and support the firm's strategic initiatives.
5. The compensation system should be as simple to understand as possible.
6. The compensation program should not promote game playing or manipulation.
7. Compensation should be viewed as fair by the participants.
8. The compensation system should be affordable.
9. The compensation system should value group harmony more than the recognition of individual efforts.
10. The compensation system should recognize and value different individual skills.
11. The compensation system should treat all clients as clients of the firm, not clients of the individual.
12. The compensation system should value business development with existing clients and community/industry involvement as much as new client acquisition.
13. The compensation system should promote camaraderie over internal competition.
14. The compensation system should support the redistribution of work as opposed to redistribution of pay.
15. The compensation system should recognize that we value a work/life balance.
16. The compensation system should emphasize client service.
17. The compensation system should value passive business development as much as active business development.
18. The compensation system should not warp people's behavior, encourage self-interest, or create rancor in the organization.

one of the biggest challenges in developing a compensation program is gaining consensus on the underlying philosophy, but without it, no program design is likely to meet each of the principals' expectations. When there is a disconnect regarding the compensation plan, it is more often an issue of the underlying compensation philosophy than an issue of the numbers themselves.

The power of the compensation philosophy statement as a decision-making tool is also significant. Every change in a compensation plan that an organization considers needs to pass through this filter. Beyond that, the statement can be an important measurement and evaluation tool. As changes to the compensation structure are envisioned, the management team may weigh the value and likely success of suggested changes against the stated philosophy. Presumably, compensation components that conform to the stated philosophy should be considered. Changes that substantially deviate from the compensation philosophy should either be rejected or cause the principles to be revisited.

Reinforcing Behavior

Among advisers who started out in corporate environments that rewarded top producers, a tendency to look the other way when top asset gatherers behave badly can linger. This bad behavior can manifest as abuse of staff, dishonesty with clients, disrespect of management, or any number of behaviors that put the firm at risk and strain relationships to the breaking point. When compensation—including incentive pay—is tied solely to revenue production, no natural constraints on behavior are in place. Of course, compensation cannot substitute for active management, but it can be an important tool for keeping potential miscreants in check if you desire to keep them as part of your organization. Not only is it important that your compensation plan reinforce *good* behavior; it's critical that it not reinforce *bad* behavior.

Plan Affordability

Many factors affect the appropriate level of base compensation and total compensation within a firm, including external benchmarks. However, one of the risks of relying on benchmarks exclusively, without regard to the economic reality of your firm, is that you could spend yourself into oblivion. That's why it helps to relate compensation to productivity standards as well as to the firm's profitability needs. When it comes to advisory firms, the real answer to the question "How much are comparable positions paid?" is usually "As much as the business can afford." Compensation is driven as much by the economics of the business as by the "market rate" for a particular job or for the individual in the job. When affordability is of particular concern—say, in a start-up business or in a flat or declining economy—more compensation should be shifted from fixed (base) to variable (incentive) compensation, thereby sharing the risk and reward more evenly between employer and employee. But regardless of the variable/fixed makeup of the compensation, you have to make a profit after fair compensation to all staff, including yourself as the owner.

Staff Expectations

We've found that when the reward structure is out of sync with what the staff is expecting, it's usually for one of several reasons:

♦ The market dictates higher pay.
♦ The nature of the pay is not in line with the employee's needs.
♦ The employee does not have a good understanding of the total pay package.
♦ The employer and employee are not in sync regarding the job and its expectations.

More and more, we see disconnects between how the manager and the employee define the job and value the contribution, particularly when the employee is still in the process of building his or her skills. One midsize firm in the Midwest, for example, hired high-level employees with ten to fifteen years of experience in other branches of the industry (brokerage, insurance) at a $30,000 salary, with expectations of developing them into financial planners. Although the employer's expectation was that the planners' compensation and responsibilities would grow slowly over time, as they would for a brand-new planner right out of school, these experienced professionals expected that they would be up to speed after the first year, meeting with clients, and receiving much greater compensation, with the goal of making $100,000 within eighteen months. To avoid these detrimental disconnects, the career path, expectations, and resulting compensation need to be clearly outlined and communicated.

The structure of the compensation—the *how*—can also be the source of a potential disconnect between employer and employee. One firm, for example, asked us to review its phantom-stock plan to make sure it related well to its strategy. In the course of our interviews with the staff, we found that most felt they were being paid at below-market rates and were more concerned about making mortgage and car payments than having a big payoff tied to their retirement or the sale of the business. As firms get more sophisticated, they're often tempted to make their compensation plans more complex simply for the sake of sophistication. These plans are often devised without input from staff on their real needs or preferences regarding the nature and form of their compensation. Ask your staff what they need and what they want. This is always a good starting point and can be closely related to the considerations of affordability to the business, behavior reinforcement, and alignment with the business strategy.

The Components of Compensation

Compensation plans at advisory firms wander all over the map. Some are 100 percent variable; others are 100 percent fixed. But all compensation programs have five components, or five buckets (see *Figure 7.1*), among which each organization strikes a different balance:
1. Base pay
2. Bonuses and incentives
3. Benefits
4. Perquisites
5. Long-term wealth building

Base Compensation

Base pay is fair market compensation for the role the individual performs, based on job duties, regardless of whether the individual is an owner or employee. Later in this chapter, we'll describe the process of establishing base pay. Base pay is typically *fixed* pay; com-

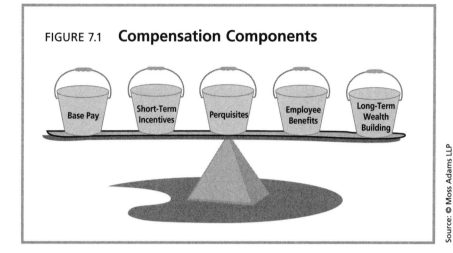

FIGURE 7.1   **Compensation Components**

Base Pay · Short-Term Incentives · Perquisites · Employee Benefits · Long-Term Wealth Building

Source: © Moss Adams LLP

mission-based pay is essentially *variable* base pay. Like fixed base pay, commission-based pay is the amount an individual gets paid for doing his or her job. The more an individual's performance is tied to revenue generation, the more contingent on short-term variables that person's pay should be. The more an individual's role is related to processes or administration, the more fixed his or her compensation should be. But there are variations on these themes, depending on the type of culture and organization you're trying to create.

Bonuses and Incentives

A bonus or incentive is an amount over and above base pay that should be awarded when the business or individual achieves certain milestones or exceeds expectations. Too many advisory firms pay a bonus, rather than an incentive. A bonus is usually a surprise; it is not typically tied to any measurable expectation and tends to be discretionary. An incentive, on the other hand, links performance and behavior to the pay. It's important when setting up incentive programs to measure and reward the right types of performance and not merely achievement of the ordinary or expected.

In compensating a professional adviser, it's typical to have some amount of compensation "at risk"—incentive pay based on the performance of either the firm or the individual (or both). The theory is that incentive pay motivates a certain kind of behavior (determined by how you structure the incentive plan) and that incentive pay allows you to strike the desired balance of risk between the professionals and the organization.

Most firms that do not have incentive pay omit it either by neglect or because they do not know what to measure. In some cases, the reluctance seems to stem more from the desire not to judge or distinguish one individual's performance or contribution from another's at the risk of saying one is "better than" and the other is "worse than." Some firms are reluctant to say that one person's skill set is more or less valued than another's, or that someone's performance is better or worse, or that someone's contribution is bigger or smaller. This kind of equanimity is not necessarily a bad idea; in fact, it's core to the culture at some firms. It will, however, affect the compensation program design significantly.

The factors that would potentially drive an incentive program are those things that matter to the organization, including but not limited to:

♦ Individual job performance
♦ Firm performance
♦ Tenure
♦ Saturation of a target market
♦ Attainment of certifications or education
♦ Business-development responsibility
♦ Special contributions

Benefit Plans

Benefit plans are put in place by employers to support cash compensation. They may include health insurance, disability and life insurance, and 401(k) plans. These sweeteners in compensation are often necessary to compete for talent, though small businesses must be careful about trying to offer plans competitive with larger organizations that can afford to offer more.

Perquisites

Perquisites are also noncash benefits—for example, a club membership or a car paid for by the business—that are usually conferred on someone because of status. Senior staff people may get free parking.

These benefits are often a hidden but substantial cost in small businesses and can distort profitability if not managed well.

Long-Term Wealth-Building Plans

These plans may be tied to long-term behavior and may include options, partnership or other stock ownership, or even phantom stock. Equity-type offerings should be reserved for individuals who behave like owners and whose contributions to the business result in enhanced value. Equity should never be given; it should always be sold. It's important for participants in these programs to have some skin in the game.

Phantom stock and options, on the other hand, may be issued to key people as a form of noncash compensation. In both cases, the employees realize the benefit when the business is sold, or in some cases, when they retire. Typically, these forms of equity protect the current owners from income dilution and loss of ownership control and do serve a role in some practices. However, most advisory firms should validate how important such synthetic equity is to the employee compared with real ownership. In many cases, for example, it's not the idea of equity that's so compelling but the ego fulfillment that comes from saying, "I'm a partner."

Establishing Base Compensation

Setting the base compensation can be a challenge. Should it be fixed or variable? What is the person's contribution, responsibility, experience? What does the market pay? Base compensation is the amount an employee gets paid for doing his job. Such compensation can be paid in essentially three ways:

- ◆ **Fixed salary:** Market-rate compensation, paid as a fixed base salary
- ◆ **Commission:** Pay for doing the job, commission is paid on a variable basis instead of a fixed basis (a hybrid between base and incentive compensation)
- ◆ **Draw:** Base pay for the job, calculated as a percentage of the individual's previous year's total compensation

The most common form of base pay—used in combination with incentive pay or in isolation—is a fixed salary, which is the simplest and most "firm-oriented" of the above options. The process of establishing base pay should take into consideration:

◆ The job description and responsibilities
◆ Market compensation benchmarks as a baseline
◆ Adjustments to market-rate compensation based on the individual's experience, tenure, and designations, as well as on affordability to the firm
◆ Annual reviews and adjustments based on changing responsibilities or expectations

This process, of course, begs the question, What *is* market-rate compensation?

Benchmarking Compensation

One benchmark that owners of advisory practices often ask us to consider in our compensation studies is a job title's *market rate*—defined as what the individual could earn working elsewhere, given geography, experience, and expertise. Perhaps a better way to think of market rate is not in terms of what the employee could make elsewhere but in terms of what it would cost to hire someone else to perform the employee's job. This is typically the best way to examine market rate, by asking not "What is the *candidate* worth?" but rather "What is the *job* worth?" and "What is *this* candidate worth in *this* job?"

Compensation benchmarks for jobs in financial-advisory firms are hard to come by, particularly for relationship-manager and senior-adviser positions. The biannual *FPA Compensation and Staffing Study* provides benchmarks unique to this market for a wide variety of job functions. *Figure 7.2* is an example of a detailed table for the paraplanner position from the 2003 study. Worksheet 6 in the appendix describes how to interpret these detailed tables, specifically, and presents some questions you should consider when evaluating any compensation benchmarks or salary survey data.

We often apply market-rate information to a firm attempting to align its compensation plan with its strategic plan. As a first step, to

FIGURE 7.2

PARAPLANNER

Primary Function   K

A technical position responsible for the detail work in developing modular or comprehensive financial plans for clients in support of a relationship manager. Limited client contact except in meetings, data gathering, and follow-up.

Number of positions reported: 267
% who are owners: 0.4
Median % ownership: 25.0

	<$250,000	$250,000–$500,000	$500,000–$1,000,000	>$1,000,000
Positions reported, by firm revenue	10.5%	13.9%	24.3%	51.3%

	Salary Only	Salary + Incentive	Commission Only	Ownership Distribution	Combination	No Data
Compensation method	43.1%	45.7%	0.0%	0.0%	6.0%	5.2%

Compensation information:	Lower Quartile	Median	Upper Quartile
Base compensation	$32,500	$38,000	$45,759
% reporting bonus		48.9%	
Bonus	$1,309	$3,000	$5,043
Median bonus, % median salary		7.9%	
% reporting commissions		4.9%	
Commissions	$5,000	$10,000	$21,000
% reporting ownership distribution		0.4%	
Ownership distribution	$670	$670	$670
Total compensation	$35,000	$40,000	$50,000

Factors impacting compensation: Variance as a % of median base compensation	Lower Quartile	Median	Upper Quartile
Experience (in years)	3	5	8
Variance in salary by work experience	89%	105%	139%
Tenure (in years)	1	3	5.75
Variance in salary by tenure	105%	97%	123%

provide a composite, we pull together data from a variety of sources. We try to observe industry data, local market factors, and national industry factors in evaluating a position. Obviously, it's important that the position be defined clearly so that our comparisons are relevant. The external benchmarks and internal affordability and job-worth analysis will be used to define a salary range for each position defined within the firm.

PARAPLANNER (continued)

	CFP
CFP certificate holder	14.6%
Variance in salary if CFP certificant	111%

Population of local market	<$250,000	$250,000–$1,000,000	$1,000,000+	No Data
% of positions reported by population	18.4%	23.3%	54.3%	4.0%
Variance in salary by population	83%	95%	105%	

Most common secondary functions	No Secondary	0	N, Q	Other
% reporting secondary function	49.8%	13.1%	6.4%	30.7%
Variance in salary by secondary function				
As a % of median base compensation	100%	101%	89%	
As a % of total compensation	100%	106%	94%	

Full- vs. part-time:	Full-Time	Part-Time	No Data
% of positions reported	83.5%	15.7%	0.7%

	Lower Quartile	Median	Upper Quartile
Annual salary for part-time	$19,500	$25,000	$30,000

As a general rule, you do not want to start an individual's compensation at the upper level of the range because you have nowhere to go once this salary is established, unless you want to violate your guidelines or promote the person to another position. To decide into which tier to place the person for base purposes, make a judgment based on experience and credentials, financial contribution to the firm, and responsibility. As the individual's experience, credentials, and contributions increase, he or she would be moved higher within the range each year.

If practical, renew the survey and evaluate your pay range each year, although every other year may be adequate in a normal market. Your pay ranges will likely need to be adjusted for inflation or cost of living (COLA) each year, if affordable. COLA amounts during the past few years have ranged from 3 percent to 4 percent in most markets. Changes in inflation or cost of living will be reflected in changes to the range; changes in performance expectations will be reflected by a change in the individual's position within the range. So it's possible for an individual who does not move up a tier to still receive an increase in base pay, depending on changes in inflation.

Establishing an Incentive Compensation Plan

Whereas base pay is compensation for doing the job, incentive compensation is pay for exceeding the expectations for the job. There are essentially three different ways incentives can be paid:

♦ **Incentive pay:** Performance-based pay, earned by exceeding defined personal or firm goals

♦ **Bonus:** Discretionary extra pay if the firm or individual does well, although neither term is defined up front, and a bonus is typically a surprise

♦ **Profit sharing:** Similar to incentive pay but tied solely to the firm's profitability goals, which may or may not be defined and communicated up front

There is a difference between a bonus and an incentive. A bonus is a surprise. An incentive is tied to some measurable expectation. Although a Christmas bonus is not a bad thing in and of itself, you will be disappointed if you expect it to drive behavior. It's a gift; it's not incentive pay. There is room for either or both in a compensation plan, but you need to be clear on how you're paying, why you're using a given method, and what you expect it to accomplish. Incentive pay that is tied to particular behavior will, by its very nature, be more successful in motivating defined behavior.

For an incentive plan to be effective, employees at every level need to be able to fill in the blank: "If I/we do more of _____, I will make more money." If not everyone on the staff can answer that question, the incentive plan is overcomplicated, ineffective, or nonexistent.

If an incentive plan is in place but is ineffective, one of the following is typically at fault:
♦ The plan is not well matched to the firm's style.
♦ The plan is sending conflicting messages.
♦ The plan is not understood by participants.
♦ There is too much or too little at risk.
♦ The performance measures or measurement systems are dysfunctional.

There are a number of steps to consider in designing an incentive plan:
♦ What will be the role of incentive compensation in your overall plan?
♦ What is the desired balance between risk and reward, variable and base pay?
♦ Who will be eligible and at what level?
♦ What kind of behavior are you trying to encourage?
♦ How will you evaluate and measure that behavior and performance?
♦ Are you inclined toward team-based, individual-based rewards, or both?

Before getting down to the mechanics of the plan, make sure you understand the drivers and philosophy underlying it.

The Role of Incentive Compensation in the Overall Plan

Typically, the role incentive compensation plays in a total compensation plan will vary by firm and usually by position within a firm. A number of factors affect whether a position will be eligible for incentive pay and what proportion of total compensation the incentive will represent:
♦ Relationship management (higher percentage variable pay) versus client service (lower percentage variable). Who is accountable to the client?

♦ Solving problems (higher percentage variable pay) versus analyzing problems (lower percentage variable). What is the level and nature of the work being performed?

♦ Revenue generation (higher percentage variable pay) versus facilitation of revenue generation (lower percentage variable). How much influence does the person have on business development?

♦ Hard, quantitative measures (higher percentage variable pay) versus soft, qualitative measures (lower percentage variable). How is the position's performance measured?

Those positions that have greater influence on the success of the business typically have more compensation at risk—a higher incentive portion—and also have greater upside potential. This is the risk-reward relationship at work. An administrative position might have 0–5 percent of total compensation as incentive, whereas a purely business-development position might have 50–75 percent or more of total compensation as incentive.

Determining Performance Measures

Incentive plans in the most successful firms are moving further away from strictly revenue-based drivers and working to incorporate additional measures. Although personal productivity is still measured and rewarded for professional positions in most firms, some additional performance measures driving compensation include:

♦ New clients in a target market
♦ Total firm revenue
♦ Revenue within a target market
♦ Revenue within a target product or service area
♦ Firm profitability
♦ Client satisfaction/client service
♦ Commitment to developing staff
♦ Events or milestones
♦ Special tasks or projects

We recommend having no more than five performance measures or goals per position. It's best to focus and emphasize the most important factors and have those be the ones that affect incentive compensation directly. It's also important that measures not be conflicting, too broad, or too difficult to measure or evaluate.

Communicating and Implementing the Plan

The most important thing to do first when communicating a new incentive compensation plan is to communicate the underlying philosophy. Even people who deliberately and carefully develop a plan tend to get caught up in the mechanics when they describe how it works. Before you start talking calculations and mechanics, make sure that you've clearly described the philosophy the plan is built on and how the plan relates to your overall business strategy.

Make sure that the participants in the plan will have ongoing access to performance results and feedback on how they're doing. If you reach the end of the measurement period and the results are a surprise to the participants, then the plan was not well administered during that period. Make sure managers are trained in giving feedback and conducting meaningful performance appraisals.

Do not forget that even the best compensation plan in the world will not allow you to relinquish active management.

The Role of Equity Participation

In addition to cash compensation in the form of base and incentive pay and noncash compensation in the form of benefits and perquisites, more advisory firms—particularly growing firms and those with an eye on their own retirement and succession—are examining the role of equity or other long-term wealth accumulation in the overall compensation scheme.

Long-term wealth-building plans should be tied to long-term behavior and should be reserved for those individuals who behave like owners and whose contributions to the business result in enhanced value. This ensures that you have the right people in the ownership pool and that additional owners will enhance the existing owners' value rather than dilute it.

Equity participation may be real—in the form of options, partnership, or other stock ownership—or it may be in the form of phantom stock. Real equity should always be sold, rather than given away, and the criteria for becoming an owner should be well deliberated.

Consider these questions:
- What are the thresholds to become a partner?
- What are the qualities—financial and nonfinancial—the firm is looking for in a partner?
- When can the firm afford to add a partner without diluting the income of current partners?
- What kind of partners will create value in the organization, as opposed to diluting it?
- What is the value of ownership?
- How much ownership will be shared?
- Are the other partners willing to share control?
- Are there structures in place to compensate and evaluate partners consistently?

Figure 7.3 (at right, and continuing) summarizes several equity compensation plans.

Owner's Compensation

If you're an owner and actively working in your business, which most advisory firm owners do, then this entire compensation discussion applies to you too. Owners of advisory firms should be compensated like any other person *for their role as employees of the business:* base compensation for the job they do and incentive compensation for exceeding expectations. And they should be held to the same performance expectations and evaluation process as any employee doing the same job. The third component of compensation, ownership distribution, is the piece that distinguishes owners from others who do the same job. This piece of compensation rewards the owners for the risk inherent in running a small business and should be evaluated against returns for other investments of similar risk.

Essentially, each owner should be paid:
- **Base compensation**: Market-rate compensation for the job he or she does
- **Incentive pay:** Compensation for exceeding the expectations of the job

♦ **Ownership distribution:** Return on his or her investment in the business

This practice not only enforces some discipline in the firm by having the owners paid and evaluated by the same measures as the others in the same job, it also allows the owners to effectively evaluate their own return on investment. It allows the firm to define the role of the owners, define the value of the jobs, hold each owner accountable to a level of performance, and differentiate between the rewards for labor and rewards for ownership. This also allows the owners to differentiate contributions made by different partners at different phases in their careers. Although equal partners would receive the same ownership distribution, the compensation for the role they play in the business—both base and incentive—would change over time as their job, performance, and contribution changes.

FIGURE 7.3 **Equity Compensation Plans**

NONQUALIFIED STOCK OPTIONS (NQSOs)

Description
The option to purchase shares of company stock in the future at their current (at time of grant) fair market value. To exercise the options the employee pays for the stock (in cash or previously owned stock). To derive the cash value of the shares after exercising the option to purchase them, the employee must sell them.

The option strike price can be set at the fair market value at the time of the grant, or it can be set at a discount/premium.

Example
BLT Financial LLC grants Steve the option to buy 10,000 BLT membership units @ $1.50/unit (strike price)—the fair market value of the units at the time of the grant, established by an independent valuation. The options become exercisable in five years, with 20% vesting (i.e., not subject to forfeiture) each year. If Steve leaves the firm, he forfeits all nonvested options.

Advantages to firm
♦ The employee has a strong incentive to contribute to the appreciation of the firm's value.
♦ Gives the employee the equivalent of ownership but *not* the right to participate in ownership decision (until options are exercised).
♦ Usually tied to staying with the firm for a period of time (vesting)— long-term incentive.
♦ Can result in significant benefit to the employee without a major cash outlay to the firm.
♦ A tax deduction at exercise.

Advantages to employee
Potentially significant gain and a share of the prosperity of the firm.

Disadvantages to firm
Results in dilution of the shares (i.e., there are more shares after the exercise "sharing" the same total value).

Disadvantages to employee
♦ Can result in a tax liability without providing the cash to pay for it.
♦ The exercise of the options gives the employee shares of stock, *not* cash. If the firm is private, turning the shares into cash can be very difficult.
♦ In a private firm, it may be difficult to establish the fair market value of the shares and, correspondingly, the strike price and exercise price.

Tax implications
♦ At the time of exercise, the difference between the strike price and the fair market value of the stock is considered ordinary income to the employee. Notice that tax is owed even if the stock is not sold—a cash flow issue.
♦ The company can take a deduction equal to the income to the employee.

INCENTIVE STOCK OPTIONS (ISOs)

Description
Substantially the same as NQSOs but receive different tax treatment. To qualify

for such treatment:

—A formal plan must be put in place and approved by the board.

—Exercise price must equal strike price.

—Plan is offered to employees only.

—There is a maximum dollar grant per year.

Example

◆ Under its ISO plan, BLT Financial LLC grants Steve the option to buy 10,000 BLT membership units @ $1.50/unit (strike price)—the fair market value of the units at the time of the grant, established by an independent valuation.

◆ The options become exercisable in five years, with 20 percent vesting (i.e., not subject to forfeiture) each year. If Steve leaves the firm, he forfeits all nonvested options.

Advantages to firm

Advantages to the employee (hopefully) translate into better performance.

Advantages to employee

Significant tax benefit compared with NQSOs.

Disadvantages to firm

◆ No tax deduction unless a disqualifying disposition is made.

◆ Must comply with the IRS requirements.

Disadvantages to employee

Some restrictions on selling in the first year after exercise if the employee wants to use the tax benefit.

Tax implications

◆ No income tax is owed at option grant and exercise, *but* the spread between fair market value and strike price can trigger alternative minimum tax.

◆ The taxable event is the sale of the shares. If shares are held for two years from the date of the grant *and* one year from exercise, gain is taxed as capital gain.

◆ If holding criteria are not met, the spread between the strike price and the exercise price is treated as ordinary income and the difference between exercise price and sale price is a capital gain.

♦ No tax deduction to the company *unless* the employee sells the shares earlier (disqualifying disposition).

PHANTOM STOCK

Description
Fictional units equivalent to shares of stock are granted to employees. The value of the units mirrors the appreciation of the company shares, valued at a given date.

Example
BLT Financial LLC grants Steve 10,000 phantom units. At the time, an independent valuation established the fair market value of the membership units of BL to be $1.50/unit. Over the next five years the stock appreciates to $5.00. At the end of the five years Steve receives 10,000 units @ $3.50/unit = $35,000.

Advantages to firm
Provides the employees with an equity-equivalent incentive without giving them a vote in the firm as shareholders.

Advantages to employee
♦ Avoids the cost of having to finance the options—e.g., Steve would have had to come up with $15,000 to exercise the options.
♦ Typically accrues dividend equivalent to that paid to common shares.

Disadvantages to firm
A cash outlay to the company. Payment can be made in stock, but then why not use options?

Disadvantages to employee
♦ No flexibility in when to exercise the phantom stock.
♦ Loss of any subsequent appreciation.

Tax implications
♦ On payment date, the value of the units is ordinary income to the employee.

♦ The company takes a deduction for the same amount as the employee's income.

STOCK APPRECIATION RIGHTS (SARs)

Description
The employee receives a payment equal to the difference between a stated strike price and the fair market value at the time of the exercise. Unlike phantom stock, SARs remain exercisable over a period of time, rather than valued at a certain date.

Example
BLT financial grants Steve SARs equivalent to 10,000 units. The strike price is $1.50/unit. Over the next five years the units appreciate to $5.00. At the end of the five years Steve receives 10,000 units @ $3.50/unit = $35,000.

Advantages to employee
♦ Greater flexibility of exercise than with phantom stock.
♦ Often granted in conjunction with options to allow the employee to have cashless exercise.

Disadvantages to firm
Significant cash outlay at exercise.

Tax implications
♦ The value of rights is taxed as ordinary income to employee only when exercised.
♦ Company takes a corresponding deduction when rights are exercised.

RESTRICTED STOCK

Description
An award of nontransferable stock to an employee that is subject to substantial forfeiture risk. The restrictions are lifted over a period of time or lapse gradually.

Example

BLT Financial grants Steve 10,000 restricted membership units. The units are not transferable, do not accrue dividends and are forfeited if Steve leaves the firm in the next five years. At the end of the five years the transferability restriction is lifted.

Advantages to employee

◆ If the shares do not appreciate, stock options, SARs, and phantom stock are all worthless. Restricted stock still has value.

◆ The employee becomes a shareholder immediately, with voting and other rights.

Disadvantages to firm

◆ The employee appears to get something for nothing, especially if he/she is a new recruit.

◆ The employee becomes a shareholder immediately with voting and other rights.

Tax implications

The employee can elect to be taxed at the time of the award or at the time the restrictions lapse. The election needs to be made within 30 days of grant. The amount of the award (i.e., value at the grant date or value at restriction lapse) is taxed as ordinary income.

STOCK PURCHASE PLAN

Description

The opportunity to purchase shares of the company at a discount to fair market value or at book value. Shares bought may be a separate nonvoting class. The company may also "make a market" by buying back shares at a predetermined formula to provide liquidity.

Example

BLT Financial LLC offers a membership purchase plan for its key employees. At the end of each year, the company gives Steve the opportunity to purchase up to $100,000 worth of membership units valued at (5 × EBITDA)/number of outstanding units. At retirement, the company will buy the units back at the same valuation formula.

Advantages to firm
♦ Receives fair market value for the shares.
♦ Presents ownership as a privilege rather than a right.

Disadvantages to firm
No tax advantages

Disadvantages to employee
May lack resources to participate adequately or be reluctant to participate if they feel that they do not have full control over the future of the company

Tax implications
♦ The discount, if any, is treated as ordinary income. The gain on the shares after the purchase is capital gain.
♦ The company gets no deduction, unless the shares are sold at discount.

PERFORMANCE SHARES

Description
A set of shares granted for reaching predefined goals. The number of shares can vary depending on the performance parameters. The period for measuring performance can be designed to be longer than a year (for example, 5 years).

Example
BLT Financial LLC offers an ownership bonus plan for its key employees. Steve will receive 10,000 units if he exceeds his revenue target for the year and an additional 1,000 shares for every $100,000 above his target.

Advantages to firm
♦ The award is tied to concrete goals that are clear and measurable.
♦ The award is contingent on individual (team) performance but the value of

the shares relies on the value of the entire company—a good combination of individual and company goals.

Disadvantages to firm
It may be difficult to anticipate the cost of the program in terms of dilution to other shareholders.

Disadvantages to employee
♦ The shares are likely illiquid.
♦ Tax liability regardless of sale.

Tax implications
The value of the stock award is treated as ordinary income and the company can take a deduction.

Financial Management

ATTRACTING CLIENTS, adding assets, and generating revenue are how most financial advisers measure their financial success as practitioners. In reality, financial success is defined by profitability, strong cash flow, a healthy balance sheet, fair return for the owner, and value that's transferable. Unfortunately, many financial advisers are in the dark about these matters. That's because the process so many financial-advisory firms have in place for accounting is inadequate, and most practitioners have not been trained to use their financial data to effectively manage their businesses. But used properly, financial information can help owners and managers identify problems more quickly, recognize trends, and take action that will transform their practices into elite financial-advisory firms.

Fundamentals of Accounting

Financial advisers understand some concepts in finance and accounting quite well, but we find that they tend to get lost in the little pictures. Financial statements are often loaded with details, making it difficult to observe trends.

Laying a solid foundation for effective financial management means building financial statements with the end user in mind, then constructing backup details to support those statements. Disbursements and receipts are recorded in a general ledger; the general ledger is then translated into a financial statement. Is this work too much of a burden on a small-business owner? No, not with the availability of inexpensive accounting-software tools and capable bookkeepers. Although the process does add temporarily to your administrative costs, the insight you obtain will help you become a more effective decision maker. Furthermore, accounting and financial management are fundamental to running any business. You're making an investment of time, money, management, and energy. Do you recommend investments for your clients without understanding how that money will be deployed or how the return should be realized? Without a clear understanding of the unique financial dynamics of your practice, there is no way to know if you're doing things right.

One advisory firm we worked with had grown its top line 15–20 percent a year for four years in a row. When we met the owner, his practice was generating $3 million in annual revenues; his take-home pay was $75,000. He was thrilled by the top line but couldn't figure out why he was making so little. If you were he, wouldn't you want to know how to evaluate your results before continuing such a growth plan?

This chapter reviews the fundamentals of accounting so that we can demonstrate effective financial-management techniques. We defer to the bookkeepers and accountants (and accounting textbooks) on the actual entries into a general ledger and how they're translated into a financial statement. But we provide some essentials regarding what should be tracked on your financial statements and which details should be kept separate so that you can dig deeper into the questions that may arise. You'll also find in the appendix a sample chart of accounts and other forms in worksheets 7 through 10. The goal is to offer a management guide, not a bean counter's how-to. Having a solid understanding of the financial dynamics of your business can be one of the most useful management tools for understanding which strategic and operations decisions the data point to.

Constructing a Financial Statement

Every month, every financial-advisory firm should produce three financial statements:

1. A balance sheet
2. An income statement (also known as the P&L, or profit and loss statement)
3. A statement of cash flow

These statements are interrelated, but each is important in its own right. Although each of the statements is about something different, together they provide the complete story on the underlying economics of a practice. Unfortunately, most owners of advisory firms regard the balance sheet as a cover page and the income statement as a scorecard. They look to either the bottom line or the top line to see how it tallies and then file the statement away. When you understand how rich this information is, you will likely begin to view the data quite differently. We know that the accounting side of a business can be mind numbing for business owners—even financial advisers who deal with numbers every day. But once mastered, the language will come naturally to you.

The Balance Sheet

One reason the balance sheet is unappreciated by most advisers—or by most service-business owners, for that matter—is it gives the false perception that a firm has very few assets (in terms of current and fixed assets, as opposed to assets under management). In many cases, not all of the firm's assets are recorded. In other cases, the method of accounting forces the balance sheet to be bypassed altogether.

Typical items left off the balance sheet include work in process (WIP), prepaid fees (retainers) and prepaid expenses, certain fixed assets, and shareholder loans. They may be omitted because the firm lacks an effective means of tracking the data or because it uses cash-basis accounting instead of the accrual method to prepare the financial statements.

One adage people like to cite in describing a balance sheet is that it tells you what you own and what you owe. This is somewhat of a misconception. The balance sheet tells you what you own and how you fund it. Assets are funded with a combination of liabilities and equity. The more a financial-advisory firm grows, the more its balance-sheet assets grow. Since all balance sheets are supposed to bal-

FIGURE 8.1   **Balance Sheet**

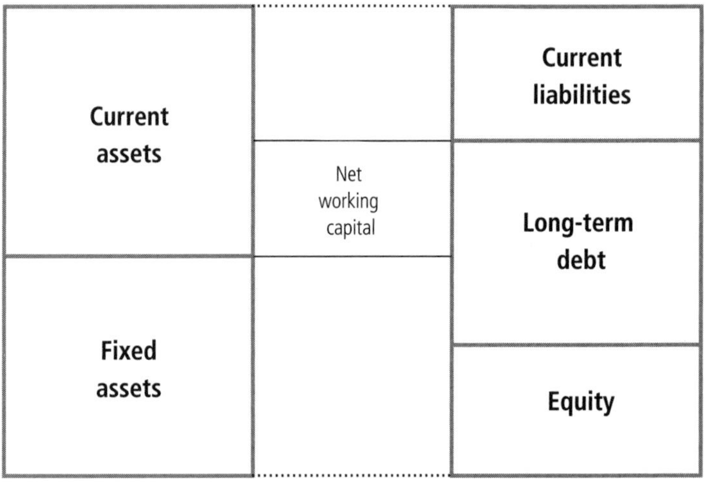

Source: © Moss Adams LLP

ance, it also becomes necessary for the funding side to grow. How will you fund your balance sheet—with equity or with debt? If debt, what kind? If equity, where will that equity come from? Let's look at some possible answers.

Worksheet 7 in the appendix provides an industry standard balance-sheet chart of accounts for your use, summarized in *Figure 8.1*. On the left side of the balance sheet are the assets. They're separated into two categories: current assets and fixed assets.

Current assets. Current assets convert to cash in one year or less and include cash, accounts receivable, and WIP. Work in process is unbilled revenue and is recognized as an asset when you perform bill-able work for a client but have not yet invoiced for it—in other words, the asset will eventually turn into cash when billed and collected (see "Work in Process," at right). Prepaid expenses also appear as a current asset and are reduced as an asset as they are applied, such as an annual prepaid insurance premium that's recognized in part each month.

Fixed assets. Fixed assets do not convert to cash and generally include furniture and fixtures, leasehold improvements, equipment, and other assets that are necessary for the operation of the business.

Occasionally, you'll also find personal assets like automobiles, airplanes, and condos on a business's financial statements. Such assets may be found on the balance sheet even when the assets are leased, which, obviously is incorrect accounting (the lessor, not the business, owns the asset). Intangible assets such as copyrights, trademarks, and goodwill may be carried on the balance sheet, though there are certain accounting rules for recognizing these assets, which an accountant can explain.

Assets are placed on a balance sheet in order of liquidity, with the most liquid assets at the top and the least liquid at the bottom. On the right side of the balance sheet are the funding sources. In a business, you fund your assets with a combination of liabilities (debt) and equity. The right side generally has three components: current liabilities, long-term debt, and equity.

Work in Process

WORK IN PROCESS (WIP) is a part of all service businesses. WIP occurs in a financial-advisory firm when you do planning for a fee or in expectation of producing other fees from the client once the planning and consulting work is done. But most financial-advisory firms have no way to account for the work because they do not track time related to client engagements. In accounting language, WIP represents unbilled revenue and is carried on the balance sheet as a current asset. Once WIP is billed, it becomes part of accounts receivable. Typically WIP is recorded when a firm tracks its time and can assign the value of its time to this asset. WIP can also be recognized on a percentage-of-completion basis.

It's important to track WIP because the work consumes a lot of cash. In a financial-advisory firm's working-capital cycle, the firm gets the client first, then it produces the work, bills for the service, and collects the fee. Current assets, not including cash itself, comprises prepaid fees, accounts receivable, and WIP. As a business grows and has new clients and new activity, accounts receivable and WIP should also grow. Since a balance sheet needs to balance, you must find a way to fund this growth in assets. Should you use debt or equity?

Current liabilities. Current liabilities are short-term obligations; they're bills that are due in one year or less. They include accounts payable, the current payments due on long-term debt, and notes payable (amounts due on a line of credit, for example). Retainers or prepaid fees would also be treated as a current liability because you have an obligation to earn those fees over the period they're being accrued; prepaid asset-management fees would typically be amortized over a quarter. A retainer fee might be amortized over the full year.

Long-term debt. This debt is an obligation due in more than one year, typically including mortgages, term loans for equipment financing, and obligations for purchases of other practices. Sometimes shareholder loans are categorized as long-term debt, but in reality such loans should be counted as equity because they rarely are paid back to the shareholder.

Equity. Equity is the shareholders' investment in the business and is also a critical part of funding the assets. Equity can come from only two sources: new capital or retained earnings (profits kept in the practice rather than distributed to the owners). Most practices begin with a nominal amount of new capital invested by the founder. New shareholders may also contribute to capital. When earnings (or profits) are retained in the business, equity grows. When the business shows net losses instead of profits, equity shrinks.

Many people presume that equity is determined by the difference between assets and liabilities. Although this is mathematically correct, the calculation tends to distort judgment about how a healthy balance sheet is built. In other words, using this definition, people often erroneously assume that if they increase their assets, they will have more equity. In reality, when the asset side of the balance sheet grows, the funding side must grow as well. So if the business does not show a profit and the owner does not contribute more capital, the only way the funding side can grow is by increasing the debt.

What's most important to understand is that *revenues drive asset growth*. The more a business grows, the more its balance-sheet assets will grow. A firm will require more furniture and fixtures, more equipment, more office space—and if it accounts for these things, its accounts receivable and WIP will also grow. If the business fails to achieve profitability, or if earnings are not retained in the business, the only way to fund the increases in assets is by borrowing more money from the bank, from a creditor, or from the owner(s). This is often the point at which owners take money out of their own pockets to put back into the practice, but emotionally and financially, this can cause a strain on the owner(s).

The Income Statement

Most advisers are familiar with an income, or P&L, statement because it's the tool they use to keep score. However, we've found that it's undervalued as a management tool because practitioners do not know how to interpret key components of this important document.

The most common format for an adviser's income statement is:

> Revenue
> − Expenses
> ―――――――
> = Owner's income

This approach may work if all you want to know is the score, but it is completely inadequate if you're trying to manage a business. Such shortcuts are as inefficient for a sole practitioner as they are for a larger firm. To begin with, the income statement should be broken into five critical elements:

> Revenue
> − Direct expense
> ―――――――――
> = Gross profit
> − Overhead expenses
> ―――――――――――
> = Operating profit

Worksheet 8 in the appendix provides an industry standard income-statement chart of accounts for your use, displayed graphically in *Figure 8.2* on the following page.

Revenue. The dollar amount that flows into your practice from all business activities—including all fees and commissions—is revenue. For example, firms affiliated with a broker-dealer would record revenues net of the broker-dealer's house fees. Firms that use a custodian and assess a planning or asset-management fee would record total receipts.

FIGURE 8.2   **Income Statement**

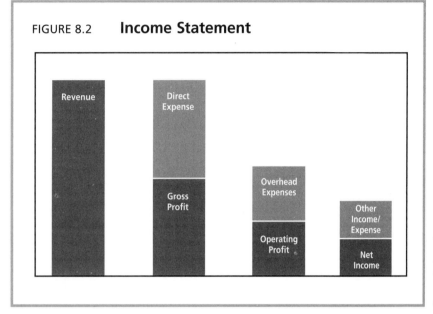

Source: © Moss Adams LLP

Direct expenses. A direct expense is defined as the reward for professional labor and should include base compensation for professional staff, whether fixed (salary) or variable (commission or incentive) compensation. Direct expenses should also include any referral fees or commissions paid to internal or external sources of business development (CPA referral fees, et cetera). The professional staff salaries should include fair-market compensation to the owner for the work the owner does as an adviser. If you're a sole practitioner, this would be an appropriate way to categorize fair-market compensation for yourself. To better understand what this "reward for labor" should be, see chapter 7 on compensation. While individual incentive payments are included in direct expense, profit sharing, which comes out of the bottom line, is accounted for in the other expense category on the income statement.

Gross profit. The amount left over after direct expenses are paid is the gross profit. Pay attention to this amount because it is what you use to cover your overhead expenses and produce an operating profit. If the gross profit is insufficient to do either, your business will be in big trouble.

Overhead expenses. Overhead expenses are all general and administrative expenses such as rent, utilities, marketing, management, administrative, and support staff, benefits, etc.

Operating profit. Operating profit is what's left over after all expenses are paid. This is also known as return on revenue, or return on sales. Different people refer to this number in different ways; operating profit is sometimes referred to as operating income or earnings. For your purposes, you should think of operating profit as your reward for ownership. Later we'll explain two other important concepts: return on investment (ROI) and return on assets (ROA).

It may also be appropriate to add lines for other income/expenses to the extent that this item is relevant in your practice; you might add a line for taxes if your business is a taxable entity such as a C corporation in the United States. An example of other income might be rental income or a special distribution; an example of other expenses might be an amount paid to settle a claim. Operating profit should record the net from operations and should not be cluttered with nonoperating income and expenses.

The primary reason for categorizing your income statement this way is to help you become a more effective financial manager for your business. By using a consistent chart of accounts, consistent language, and a consistent interpretation of the data, you'll be able to compare your firm meaningfully to other practices and to its own historical performance and identify where you may be having problems. But one problem with many advisory-firm income statements is that advisers overload each category with details instead of presenting the statements in key summary form. For example, the overhead expense numbers often include every single disbursement, no matter how small, and every person's monthly salary. Many of these lines should be presented in summary so that the financials tell the broader story first. Details are important but should be contained in backup documents in the event you need to drill deeper.

Accrual versus Cash-Basis Accounting

Cash-basis accounting. Most advisory firms prefer to use cash-basis accounting because it's simpler in some respects, although it does not always accurately reflect the economics of the practice. In cash-basis accounting, you recognize revenues when received and expenses when paid. The method is much like balancing a personal checkbook—you either have the money or you don't. For most practices, cash-basis accounting is appropriate for tax purposes but not for managing finances.

Accrual accounting. Accrual accounting allows a firm to measure profitability more accurately because it matches up the revenues and expenses to appropriate time periods. With accrual accounting, you recognize the revenues when earned even though the services may not have been paid for yet. More likely, clients have prepaid if the firm assesses quarterly payments based on assets under management. You recognize expenses when incurred, even though you may not yet have paid for them. On the revenue side, if staff members are working on a financial plan, for example, they record their time and you recognize the revenue in that time period. This revenue is matched to their monthly salaries, so that you can evaluate whether you're producing a profit on their labor. If you're not, you can take corrective action when the problem becomes chronic or a trend is indicated.

Tax management versus financial management. Please do not confuse your financial statements with your tax returns. They have different purposes and different formats. Tax returns provide very little insight into what's going on in your business from a financial-management perspective. People joke about having two sets of books, but in reality, that practice is legitimate—one set is for taxes, the other is for financial management. Most advisory firms use cash-basis accounting if they're eligible to do so, because it's usually beneficial from a tax standpoint; however, it's prudent to consider accrual accounting for your management reports, because that method gives you more insight into your business operations.

The Statement of Cash Flow

The statement of cash flow is possibly the most important but least used document in a firm's financial management. Its purpose is to show how cash is produced and consumed in a business. Its value is that it links together the balance sheet and income statement to produce a revealing story about the business. The statement of cash flow has three main components: operating cash flow, investing cash flow, and financing cash flow.

Operating cash flow. The sum total of the cash flow produced or consumed in the business from internal operations is called operating cash flow. It measures the effect on cash from operating profits and losses, depreciation (which is a noncash expense), and changes in current assets and current liabilities.

Investing cash flow. Investing cash flow is the sum total of cash used to invest in fixed assets. Unless the asset is sold, this component is rarely a positive number. Operating cash flow and investing cash flow track how the business consumes or produces cash internally.

Financing cash flow. The external sources of cash, such as bank financing or an equity infusion, are called financing cash flow. When you tally the net numbers from operating cash flow and investing cash flow, you arrive at a sum called cash flow before financing. If cash flow before financing is negative, then the firm will have to raise cash from an outside source—such as bank financing or an equity infusion.

To understand the concept of cash flow, it's important to recognize the economic dynamics of increases or decreases in assets and liabilities. When assets go up, cash goes down; when assets go down, cash goes up. When liabilities go up, cash goes up; and when liabilities are paid down, cash goes down (see *Figure 8.3*). A sample statement of cash flow is provided in worksheet 10 in the appendix.

This cash-flow phenomenon explains why so many small-business owners can't understand why their cash disappears when their businesses grow. A growing business adds assets; therefore, it tends to consume cash. Even service-based advisory firms experience this phenomenon. When the practice grows, advisers add balance-sheet

FIGURE 8.3   **Cash Flow Dynamics**

Assets ▲   Cash ▼   Liabilities ▲   Cash ▲

Assets ▼   Cash ▲   Liabilities ▼   Cash ▼

assets such as leasehold improvements, computers, and office furniture—and in some cases, work in process and accounts receivable.
These activities consume cash. They also tend to cause the owners of
advisory firms to borrow money from a bank or to infuse their own
cash into the business, hence the term *financing cash flow*.

Tying the Financials Together

As you'll see from the discussion on financial analysis in the next
chapter, the three financial statements are linked. Adding assets or
liabilities directly affects cash flow; profits or losses directly affect
the balance sheet. It's possible to have cash and no profits, and it's
possible to have profits and no cash. The relationship between the
two depends on whether your business is growing or shrinking and
whether you're paying attention to the fundamentals of financial
management when you evaluate your success.

There are times when it's acceptable to have the relationship
between profits and cash out of whack, as long as the condition is not
chronic. But in the long term, the goal should be to achieve harmony
in your financial statements. That harmony is measured by:

♦ A healthy balance sheet
♦ Strong cash flow
♦ Increasing profits
♦ Fair return to the owner

As you begin to apply discipline to the financial management
of your practice, you will also begin to see how such discipline
affects your ability to provide the ultimate client-service experience.
A growing, profitable enterprise has the financial resources to reinvest in the knowledge, technology, and tools that will make it easier
for clients to do business with it. Furthermore, having a financially
successful enterprise will help ensure that your focus as an adviser is
on your work and not on your own financial needs.

(and Other Dirty Words)

THE FINANCIAL-ADVISORY business has entered a phase of rapid growth. For the typical firm, that growth imposes multiple demands on the professional staff's time, puts more pressure on fees, and strains owner-advisers to the limit of their capacity. By observing how these factors affect your profitability, you can make better judgments about which clients to serve, which products and services to offer, what to charge if you have control over the fees, and who in your organization needs coaching to become more effective and efficient in their work. But quantifying the problem is only half the solution. Only by seeing the trends in your financial performance can you uncover the specific questions you need to answer.

Owners of financial-advisory practices—like those of most companies—usually speak in financial terms when they describe what's going wrong with their business. But issues related to profitability, cash flow, and balance-sheet strength may in fact be the symptoms rather than the problem. Getting to the root cause involves learning how to recognize the symptoms and what they truly indicate. Such understanding begins with an analysis of your financial statements. Are they organized in a way that provides insight? Are there benchmarks that you can compare your numbers with? Are you able to observe any trends? The process for analyzing financial statements in a way that helps you evaluate what's really going on in your business isn't mysterious. It's logical and linear.

The process depicted in *Figure 9.1* allows you to quickly assess problems and observe patterns. By converting numbers into ratios,

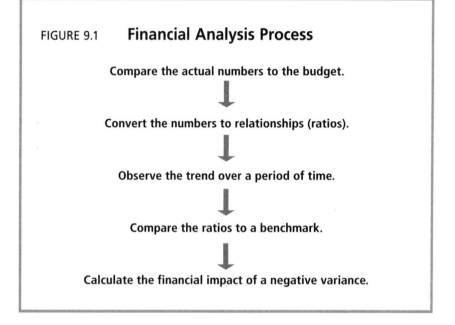

FIGURE 9.1   **Financial Analysis Process**

Compare the actual numbers to the budget.

Convert the numbers to relationships (ratios).

Observe the trend over a period of time.

Compare the ratios to a benchmark.

Calculate the financial impact of a negative variance.

you can see critical relationships as they evolve and develop a plan to improve them. By calculating the financial impact of negative variances, you can measure the magnitude of the problem. This chapter explains a thoughtful, structured, analytical process that you can use to perform triage on an ailing business.

Formatting the Financials

To better understand the assessment process, you'll need to organize your firm's financial statements in a way that makes it easier to interpret results. At a minimum, you should have a balance sheet and an income statement as described in chapter 8 on financial management and outlined in worksheets 7 and 8 in the appendix. Larger practices—especially those that use an accrual basis of accounting—should also produce a statement of cash flow. For this purpose, you'll also want to generate financial statements for back-to-back years, ideally three years and optimally five.

Analyzing the Income Statement

The income statement is the most revealing document in a financial-advisory practice because it helps you to quickly identify and address potential problems. As with the balance sheet, it's most helpful to analyze trends in the income statement over a period of time.

Classify your revenue, expenses, and profits appropriately. This helps you isolate the management issues such as poor productivity, poor pricing, or poor cost control. Observing the ratios in relationship to a benchmark and to a trend over several periods will help put the problem into context. Use industry benchmarks, such as those published by the Financial Planning Association, or other relevant industry standards that may be published by the CFA Institute, the Securities Industry Association (SIA), or the Risk Management Association (RMA). Your firm's best year or some other objective target also makes a good benchmark or goal. Let's look at *Figure 9.2*, an example of an income statement.

The income statement in Figure 9.2 indicates a practice that generates $1,000,000 in revenue. Let's assume it has one owner; one other financial adviser, who is an associate; and four support staff. The salaries of the owner and financial adviser are charged to direct expense; the support-staff salaries are considered part of overhead expenses. In this example, $250,000 is left over in operating profit, which the owner can choose to retain in the business, distribute as profit sharing to the staff, or pay out to himself as a dividend. This amount—over and above his base compensation for labor—is the

---

FIGURE 9.2 **Income Statement**

Revenue	$1,000,000	100%
Direct expenses	400,000	40
Gross profit	600,000	60
Overhead expenses	350,000	35
Operating profit	250,000	25

reward he receives in recognition of the special risks he takes as the owner of the enterprise.

Gross Profit Margin

Measuring gross profit is a foreign concept for many advisers because owners of advisory practices tend to pay themselves what's left over after all expenses are paid in the business. We refer to this as the "book of business" syndrome, and it's seen among practitioners who have not yet evolved from the sales model to the entrepreneurial model. In a solo practice, the gross profit margin is somewhat more difficult to measure because you typically do not have other professional staff to include under direct expenses. Also, solo practitioners can be more discretionary about what they pay themselves. But it's important to establish a standard of pay for professional staff, including yourself, to help you evaluate your business success. Three good sources for determining fair compensation are the Financial Planning Association's *Compensation and Staffing Study,* the data compiled by the CFA Institute, and www.salary.com.

Learning how to manage gross profit margin will probably be the single most important financial-management discipline you can apply to your practice. When profitability is declining, most financial advisers tend to cut costs. But cutting costs will do nothing to improve pricing or productivity or client mix. To determine the gross profit margin, divide gross profit dollars by total revenue. For example, if your gross profit dollars are $600,000 and your revenues are $1,000,000, the gross profit margin would be 60 percent. Put another way, for every dollar of revenue, you're generating 60 cents in gross profit.

Unfortunately, most practitioners use the financial statement as a scorecard rather than as a management tool. But *Figure 9.3* illustrates how you can use it to analyze profitability.

Company A is an example of a practice that has shown good year-to-year revenue growth but declining profits. Until we recast this adviser's financial statements, she was not well enough in tune with how the firm was performing as a business. Her measure of success was the increase in gross revenue, but she had a sinking feeling that she did not have much to show for it. When we examined

FIGURE 9.3   **Common Size Financial Statement**

	2002	% of Revenue	2003	% of Revenue
Revenue	$680,000	100%	$730,000	100%
Direct expense	320,000	47	380,000	52
Gross profit	360,000	53	350,000	48
Overhead expense	265,000	39	285,000	39
Operating profit	95,000	14	65,000	9

FIGURE 9.4   **Where Is the Problem?**

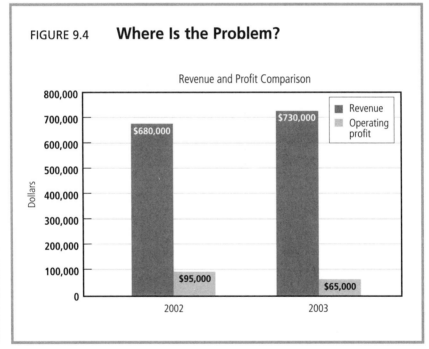

her profitability, we saw the trend illustrated in *Figure 9.4.*

When we showed the adviser Figure 9.4, illustrating revenue and profit, and asked her how she would attack the problem, instinctively, she blamed her costs. "The problem," she said, "is that everything I'm spending money on is essential." We recommended that she look more closely at her operating performance. We then showed her

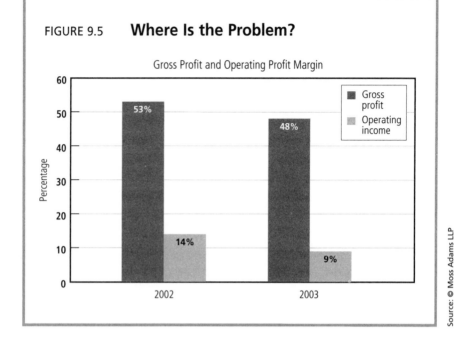

FIGURE 9.5   **Where Is the Problem?**

Gross Profit and Operating Profit Margin

Source: © Moss Adams LLP

Figure 9.5, which shows the difference between gross profit margin and operating profit margin.

As a percentage of revenue, her firm's gross profit was declining. If she were able to hold this margin level, her operating margin would stay constant as well and her operating profit *dollars* would increase. She wanted to know the cause. We found the answer by looking more carefully at how her practice had evolved during the previous year. She had added thirty new clients, most of whom were below her target fee amount. Because she did not believe that she could charge them what she normally charges for a financial plan, she had her paraplanner do the analysis at no charge to the clients. "I was taking the long-term view," she said. "I figured if I could get them on the road to saving more money, I would get a better return on investment eventually."

Certainly, her concept had merit, but it became obvious that she could not afford to take such a long-term view of new business with so many new clients. If she continued to give away her services in hopes of signing up more clients, her short-term profitability would erode to the point where she would not have the financial where-withal to support them. One unanticipated consequence of her client-development plan was having to hire another paraplanner to help support the planning and implementation process. This addition to staff raised the firm's direct expenses even more, at a time when it could not afford an increase.

This owner's plight sheds light on the dangers of taking a meat-ax to a problem that requires only a paring knife. If your gross profit margin were declining, what would you do? Had this owner decided to cut administrative staff (overhead), for example, she still would not have solved the gross-profit problem, because it was caused by poor pricing and low productivity. The key is to understand exactly what the income statement is telling you.

For example, if the gross profit margin (gross profit divided by revenue) is declining, the cause may be any one of five problems:

1. Poor pricing
2. Poor productivity
3. Poor payout
4. Poor client mix
5. Poor service/product mix

Examine your pricing. In today's market, most advisers can control what their asset-management, financial-planning, and consulting fees will be. They also control retainers and what they charge for other services that are not subject to a predetermined corporate grid. As an owner, you need to answer some key questions: Do you know how much it costs you to deliver that service or to serve that client? Do you view that service as a loss leader or as a way to enhance your profitability?

Evaluate the productivity of your professional staff. Later in this chapter, we'll provide the key ratios to apply in analyzing the performance of those who are developing business and advising clients. But in a nutshell, to evaluate productivity, you need to observe trends. Current numbers tell you a lot, but a downward movement in productivity over time sounds the alarm. Just because your gross revenues are increasing does not mean that you are building a healthy business. You can measure productivity by looking at increases in revenue per client or revenue per staff. These underlying trends are leading indicators and can tell you if you're heading into problems.

Consider your client mix. One great myth that has been carried over to the financial-advisory profession is the relevance of Pareto's constant. Pareto was an Italian economist whose studies revealed that 80 percent of the wealth was held by 20 percent of the populace. In the twentieth century, business managers began applying permutations of that concept so widely to business development that now the 80/20 rule has become an axiom in the advisory business: ergo, 80 percent of an adviser's business comes from 20 percent of the clients. Strategically, acceptance of this rule does not make sense. Why would advisers tolerate having 20 percent of their business subsidize the activities of 80 percent of their client base—or tolerate building a business that serves so many clients who are so far off their "sweet spot"? Although it may be difficult to have all of your clients fit into the optimal client profile of your business, that should still be the goal. At a minimum, the ratio should be reversed, so that 80 percent of your clients fit within the profile. If they don't, it's highly likely that the single biggest reason you're adding overhead expense is to support the large percentage of clients not in your sweet spot. If you're saying things like "I plan to add a person to serve my second- and third-tier clients," there's a problem. If they're not important enough to be served by a first-rate client-service team, why do you keep them as clients?

Evaluate your product and service mix. There is a knee-jerk tendency to add services as a favor to a client or in reaction to a perceived opportunity, but the service may not fit comfortably into the firm's existing structure or protocols as a business. Say, for example, you're asked to manage the 401(k) plan assets of a business-owner client. The process of enrolling, training, and handling a bunch of little deposits, plus the reporting, is different from the approach required in serving a high-net-worth individual. You may be expected to interact with the plan participants themselves. This may lead you to divert valuable resources by assigning a staff member to deal with this "one-off" service. You may justify providing this service as an added value to a big client, but how many of these exceptions do you have? And how do they affect the way your staff works or the way you manage quality control? Viewing your business model through the prism of revenue—and incremental revenue at that—may be harming your practice. In situations like this, employ your business strategy as your decision-making tool to ensure that the firm's product and service mix is being developed in line with the overall strategy you've committed to, rather than in a haphazard, opportunistic way (see chapter 2 on developing a long-term view).

Examine your compensation practices. Are they aligned with your business strategy? Are they suited to your market? Are you getting an adequate return on this investment? Is your professional staff contributing enough to the success of your enterprise to justify their compensation? Does your incentive plan encourage behavior that works for your business and for your clients?

Some fundamental steps are essential (see also "Productivity Analysis," page 171). Evaluate each professional staff member, or each team, to determine whether their contributions are consistent with those of other staff members or with whatever benchmark you're using. For those whose performance is below par, get them help to improve their skills or get them out. Evaluate your relationship with clients, too. Can you afford to keep all of them, or are some not netting enough revenue to cover the effort you put into managing the relationship?

Do you know what the value of your time is? Or the value of your staff's time? Are you getting paid adequately for that time? Raising prices for such things as managing or supervising assets, developing financial or estate plans, or hourly consulting is always a challenge, but especially in a tepid or mixed market. Raising prices can also have a dampening effect on increasing revenue volume. But if doing so will force you to be more selective about which clients you take, it could be a good thing. Is there anything wrong with working less and making more? Chances are you have not touched your pricing, especially for planning and consulting services, in a very long time.

When you use gross profit margin as a management tool, many improvements can result. Overhead costs are manageable. That's obvious. The silent killer is the deterioration of pricing, productivity, service mix, and client mix when you're not even aware that you're headed for trouble. It's a bit like developing high blood pressure: you feel fine until you blow a gasket. And when you do, you're more likely to become disabled than to die. Monitor these relationships, and you'll discover the root cause of most of your practice problems.

Operating Profit Margin

The operating profit margin is calculated by dividing operating profit by total revenue. For example, if your operating profit is $150,000 and your revenues are $1,000,000, your operating profit margin would be 15 percent. Expressed another way, you would be generating 15 cents of operating profit for every dollar of revenue generated. A declining operating profit margin is a sign of one or more of these three problems:

♦ A low gross profit margin
♦ Poor expense control
♦ Insufficient revenue volume

When expenses as a percentage of revenue are increasing, it should set off alarms, especially if you have a growing business. Expense control is a function of attitude. Manage expenses according to your budget, and be disciplined about writing checks or authorizing purchases that were not contemplated in the budgeting process.

Often, after a firm has a good year or two, operating profit declines because advisers go into a spending mode spurred by past success. Buoyed by the belief that the recent past will repeat itself, owners may spend money on new equipment, salaries, or rent. Inevitably, if business does not continue at the same pace, advisers find that they cannot support the new infrastructure with the revenues they're generating.

As a rule, the gross profit margin in a financial-advisory firm should be in the range of 60 percent, and operating profit margin (operating profit divided by revenue) should be in the range of 20–25 percent. This means that direct expenses should not exceed 40 percent of revenue, and overhead expenses as a percentage of revenue should not exceed 35 percent. In the event that your expenses do exceed these numbers, take steps to protect against further deterioration: understand the economics of your practice and make sure you observe the direction these numbers are taking. Note also that certain operating models require higher direct expenses and higher overhead cost—the key is to understand the economic drivers of your own business.

Break-Even Analysis

A helpful technique for determining how much you can afford to increase your infrastructure costs is called *break-even analysis*. This method helps you to determine how many additional dollars of revenue you need to generate to cover the new expenditures. Intuition may tell you that there is a one-to-one relationship, but the reality is different. You generally won't have enough revenue available to cover the increase in costs. That's because a portion of the firm's revenue dollars are going elsewhere—such as to professional salaries or, in some cases, to commissions for revenue generators.

Here's how the math works: Breakeven is determined by dividing the contribution margin into fixed costs. Traditionally, the contribution margin is determined by subtracting variable costs (direct expenses, including compensation of professional staff, whether salaries or commissions) from revenue, then dividing the difference by revenue. For example, if a firm has revenue of $400,000, variable costs (professional compensation) of $100,000, and fixed costs (overhead) of $350,000, the contribution margin is 75 percent: $400,000 – $100,000 = 300,000; $300,000 ÷ $400,000 = 75 percent contribution margin. The contribution margin is then divided into total fixed costs (overhead) to determine breakeven. So with fixed costs of $350,000, you would need to generate $466,000 ($350,000 ÷ 75 percent = $466,000) to break even.

To use break-even analysis in your practice, estimate the cost of a new staff person, for example, or the price of a piece of new equipment, then divide it by the contribution margin. If you were planning to add a new administrative staff person for $35,000, you'd divide $35,000 by the contribution margin of 0.75 and the result would be $46,666. In other words, to cover that additional $35,000 of overhead (not counting benefits), you'd need to generate an additional $46,666 in new revenue to break even.

Trend Analysis

Many advisers are inclined to look at the sum total of the income statement in isolation—apart from any trends or benchmarks. Obviously, the most relevant comparison would be to place these monthly numbers against a budget. But at least annually, advisory-practice owners should be comparing gross profit, operating profit, and overhead expenses with benchmarks and with the firm's performance in previous years. This will allow them to evaluate patterns in their business and to better assess their own performance as managers. If the numbers diverge either from those of the previous year or from the benchmarks, owners should find out why.

An effective way to manage overhead expenses is to use an exercise called *common sizing* (see Figure 9.3). Take each category of expenses and divide the dollar amount into the total revenue amount for the same period. The answer will be expressed as a percentage. For example, if the rent for the period was $36,500 and the revenue was $730,000, this would mean that rent as a percentage of revenue was 5 percent. The key to this process is comparing the trend over a period of time to observe whether "creeper" costs are evident in any single category.

Creeper costs, like coat hangers, have a way of accumulating without your knowing how. If your revenues are growing and specific expenses as a percentage of revenue are also growing, you're probably suffering from the creepers. It's not uncommon for certain costs to increase, but as a rule they should not increase as a percentage of revenue; in fact, in many cases, they should go down.

Cost control is a key element of managing to an operating profit. But so is making sure that you have sufficient revenue volume to support your infrastructure. One of the challenges of a very small practice is that a core level of infrastructure is needed to operate a business. That's why so many advisers tell us it's impossible for them to keep the expense ratio below 35 percent, and in many cases they cannot get their costs below 50 percent of revenue. If this is a chronic problem for you that is not solvable by reducing expenses, then it's time to look at how you can increase volume to support the structure. It may mean adding more productive capacity (professional staff) or merging with a firm that has natural synergies with yours.

Increasing volume basically means improving sales. The question is whether your firm has a culture of business development and the ability and unique value proposition, or branding, to attract new clients. Look back on what got you to this point to see if you can learn from past successes. Seek new referrals from all your contacts, and determine what you have to do to attract and keep clients who fit your optimal client profile.

Evaluating Return on Ownership

Unless you track your financial information, you cannot meaningfully evaluate return on ownership separately and distinctly from return on labor. Every adviser who owns and works in an advisory firm is both an employee of the business and an investor in the business and should be generating appropriate returns from both roles. If you're an employee of the business, you should be paid market-rate compensation for doing the job—*return on labor*. You should also see a *return on ownership*—typically in the form of a profit distribution—for the risk inherent in owning a business.

When the business owner is primarily responsible for revenue generation, client advice, or relationship management, the compensation for working in the business is categorized as a direct expense. When the owner's primary responsibilities are management or administration, compensation for working in the business is categorized as an overhead expense. In either case, compensation should be determined relative to the value of the job in the market.

One benchmark for setting a fair compensation level for the owner is to consider what the firm would have to pay someone else to come in and do that job. Of course, this solution doesn't take into consideration the years the owner has been with the business or the sweat and tears put into building it. Those things are recognized in the return on ownership (see *Figure 9.6*). For compensation, we're looking solely at the value of the job and what you would have to pay someone else to do it. Other good sources of compensation benchmarking data are available online and in your community, such as through Robert Half & Associates, local compensation consulting firms, or other sources. The *FPA Compensation and Staffing Study* (available at www.fpanet.org) can also provide you with industry-

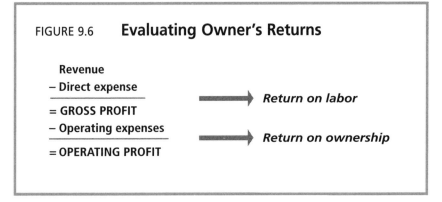

FIGURE 9.6   **Evaluating Owner's Returns**

Revenue
− Direct expense
――――――――
= GROSS PROFIT   → *Return on labor*
− Operating expenses
――――――――――   → *Return on ownership*
= OPERATING PROFIT

specific compensation benchmarks, combining job functions and levels of experience.

Analyzing the Balance Sheet

During the great tech boom, financial advisers were making money without even trying. Many got caught up in this high-flying frenzy of cigar and cognac parties and elaborate client-appreciation galas. Although these firms were producing profits, they were also consuming cash, much of it in excess staff and infrastructure. A number of advisers saw debt as a useful tool for leveraging growth. Some used it to initiate practice-acquisition programs, introduce new service lines, or build fancy offices.

As the market began its decline, the balance-sheet vice began tightening its grip on advisers. In one case, a bank asked us to help an advisory firm restructure and reorganize so that it could meet its obligations. The bank had a referral relationship with this advisory firm, as well as a lending relationship. Although the financial loss to the bank would have been considerable if the firm folded, the embarrassment to everyone involved might have been even worse. The bank required a personal guaranty on its loan to the adviser, but unfortunately for both parties, most of the adviser's assets were tied up in equity investments, which had also seen a precipitous decline.

The owner-adviser was quite resentful of our being called in, perhaps because of the personal humiliation but more likely because of his fundamental belief that he could sell himself out of

the problem. But the bank had its own regulatory and policy problems and could not let the adviser slip any further into debt. The
adviser already owed more than $500,000 and had zero equity in
the practice; cash flow was slowing and there were no assets available to pay down the loan.

Our analysis uncovered a surprising situation—and probably
one that resulted from the special relationship the adviser had
with the bank president. All of the firm's debt was in the form of
a line of credit, which, according to the bank's terms, had to be
unused, or "rested," for thirty days. In what was once a common
practice, banks would authorize a line of credit tied to something
like accounts receivable, and it would be available to fund short-
term needs. Banks often looked at service businesses as seasonal,
so they would assume that there would be a spike in borrowing as
cash got tight, then a repayment of the line when the business was
flush again. Like many advisory firms, this one assessed fees to its
clients quarterly, and so it too experienced the ebb and flow of cash
throughout the year. In this case, a market decline in asset values
materially affected cash flow.

More distressing than the declining cash flow, however, was the
use of the credit line. It appears that this owner-adviser was not buying the pessimistic adage that what goes up must come down. An
undying optimist, he saw the bear market as a tremendous opportunity to expand and did so with new offices and the buyout of another
practice, all using cash from his line of credit. In the course of our
negotiations, we were able to persuade the bank to stretch the amortization of most of the loan to five years in return for persuading
the adviser to drastically reduce his overhead, including subletting
a portion of his office space. The pain for the owner was great, but
the restructuring worked and everyone came out whole—although
it took several years before the adviser was back to an income level
that supported his lifestyle.

The moral of this story reinforces the need to understand the
power of financial leverage. Debt can be a great technique for gearing
up growth, but it carries more risk in a service business, especially
when it's structured wrong and based on a bad set of assumptions.
And this mistake may be more common than people suspect.

Although many financial advisers believe that most people in this business do not borrow to fund their operations, in our studies and consultations with advisers, we've found that not to be true. What *is* true is that many advisers simply do not have a balance sheet to monitor how they're managing assets and liabilities and, as a result, run the risk of hitting a wall. A balance sheet tells you about two things: *solvency,* a firm's ability to pay its bills; and *safety,* its ability to withstand adversity.

Solvency

Solvency is measured by comparing current assets to current liabilities, or assets that turn to cash in one year or less versus bills due in one year or less. Obviously, you always want current assets to be larger than current liabilities. By dividing current liabilities into current assets, you arrive at the current ratio. The ratio is usually expressed as a number—for example, $100,000 ÷ $50,000 = 2. This means that for every $1 of current liabilities, you have $2 of current assets. If the ratio were 0.75:1 (that is, $75,000 ÷ $100,000 = 0.75), that would mean you have $0.75 of current assets for every $1 of current liabilities.

It's best to observe this number over the course of three to five years so that you can see if there is a trend. If the number is declining, you should be aware of that. If the ratio is under 1:1, you should be worried, because it means you do not have enough current assets to cover your short-term obligations. In a distribution business, for example, it's common for companies to use a combination of long- and short-term debt. They use the short-term debt (current liabilities) to replace the cash that's tied up in accounts receivable and inventory (both current assets). When they turn over their inventory and collect on their receivables, they produce cash, which they use to pay off the short-term debt.

A financial-advisory firm can apply the same leverage, but it's important to recognize that these firms typically don't have much in current assets. Some practices have accounts receivable and also track work in process, which could convert to cash to pay off this debt. But if the firm has neither, then it runs the risk of increasing its obligations and not having a means to repay them, unless the

FIGURE 9.7   **Balance Sheet**

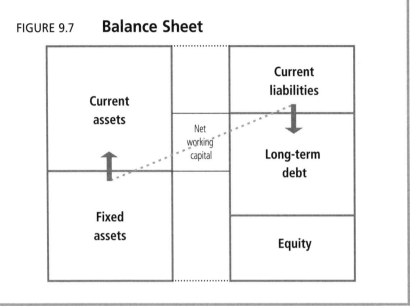

owner is willing to dig into his own pocket to pay them off.

The most common reason financial-advisory firms find themselves in a solvency squeeze is that they use short-term debt as if it were a line of credit to finance fixed assets. In the balance sheet in *Figure 9.7*, the fixed-asset line is increasing as the current liability line is dropping. The space in the middle—the net working capital—is shrinking.

The solvency squeeze occurs most frequently when a business is growing. You decide you need new office space, so you structure a new lease with more space. As part of the move, you invest in leasehold improvements to make the space appealing, and you add new furniture, fixtures, and equipment. All of these are fixed assets that need to be funded.

If you use your line of credit to purchase these fixed assets, you deplete your working capital, which you may need for critical operating expenses such as meeting payroll, settling your accounts payable to vendors, or paying quarterly taxes. A line of credit is a funding instrument designed to help a business finance its short-term operating needs, not its long-term assets. If you use up your line of credit by financing the wrong type of asset, you'll have nothing left to fund your short-term obligations.

The rule of financing is to match funding to the useful life of an asset. Long-term assets should be financed using long-term debt or equity. Short-term assets are financed using all three components—current liabilities, long-term debt, and equity. Although dipping into the credit line temporarily to purchase a long-term asset may be expedient, a lack of discipline often gets service businesses into trouble. It's a little like the client who can't stay away from the ATM machine, despite your warnings.

Safety

Safety is measured by dividing total equity into total liabilities. This is called the *debt-to-equity ratio*. The bigger the number, the more concerned you should be. Again, watch the trend over a period of time; don't just look at the number in isolation. The ratio is best expressed as follows: total debt of $100,000 divided by total equity of $50,000 = a debt-to-equity ratio of 2:1. This means you have $2 of total debt for every $1 of equity.

Most advisory firms have a debt-to-equity ratio under 1:1. When the ratio exceeds 1.5:1, there is cause for concern. Financial leverage in a service business is a very risky proposition because it usually does not have the right types of assets to fall back on to pay off this obligation. In liquidation or distress, accounts receivable and work in process get discounted to virtually nothing and fixed assets attract only a few cents on the dollar.

There are times when using debt to fund an increase in fixed assets or current assets can help accelerate the growth of the business. That should be the driving force of any borrowing you do. Obviously, if debt is used because you've been recording operating losses and have no money to fund your assets, you'll be entering a dangerous cycle.

So how do you decide when it's okay to use debt to fund growth? The principle of financial leverage is that you use debt to fund assets, which then translates into greater profitability. In a retail business, for example, the store owner will use a line of credit to purchase inventory. Once sold, the cash is used to pay down the line. In a manufacturing business, a company will use a term loan to purchase equipment that will allow it to produce its products more efficiently or in a way that helps it achieve or maintain its profitability. A financial-services business might invest in leasehold improvements, computers, or high-speed color printers and scanners, all with an eye toward enhancing the perception that it's a successful business. But will the purchase result in more business, higher-margin business, or better productivity?

Advisory firms get into trouble when they use debt to fund losses. In other words, they run out of working capital and need to pay their rent or some other expense, so they dip into their credit line. Since the borrowing is not funding an asset that helps produce profits, such a firm often finds itself in a pickle when the need to borrow occurs in every pay cycle. Having no profits means it has been unable to retain earnings to fund its growth. More debt puts an additional strain on profitability. And the cycle continues.

The Origins of Equity

When a practice grows, both its income statement and balance sheet grow with it. If the asset side of the balance sheet is growing, then the owner must use a combination of debt and equity to fund it. But equity can come from only one of two places: new capital or retained earnings.

Advisers rarely retain earnings in their practices, so to fund the increasing balance sheet, the owners of the practice might do a capital call to inject new equity into the business, or they may lend money to the business. In the eyes of a banker, by the way, a shareholder loan is treated the same as equity because it's assumed that the money will never be repaid.

If you're the owner of a small, solo practice, it's easy to put money in and take money out of the equity account, because you're accountable only to yourself. But if you're part of a larger practice with multiple stakeholders, you may find that some of your partners do not have the financial wherewithal to participate in capital calls. This puts a burden on the wealthiest shareholders and creates unnecessary conflict. So as the practice grows, begin to project your equity needs and retain earnings appropriately so that you will not have to go back to the shareholders to ask for a loan or infusion of cash for the business.

Use debt to fund the balance sheet, not to cover losses on the income statement. Recognize the principle of financial leverage, whereby debt is used to finance assets to help you produce a profit. In addition, match funding to the useful life of an asset. Be careful about using short-term lines of credit to finance long-term needs. Recognize that equity can come from only two sources and that, for both emotional and financial reasons, it's prudent to retain some earnings in your business to help fund your growth.

Analyzing the Statement of Cash Flow

Once you understand how this statement of cash flow is constructed, the analysis of cash flow becomes fairly straightforward. The most helpful cash flow ratios to observe are:

♦ Operating cash flow to revenue
♦ Operating cash flow to total assets
♦ Operating cash flow to equity

Operating cash flow is often referred to as free cash flow because it's the amount available to the owner before investment in fixed assets and before funding from outside sources. Free cash flow is a familiar concept in the valuation of an advisory firm because it's more relevant than applying a multiple to operating profit or revenue. To determine whether the business is actually producing a return, you need to know if the business is producing positive cash flow from operations. Knowing the ratio of operating cash flow to revenue, to total assets, and to equity makes you better able to evaluate the real financial returns in your business.

Operating cash flow to revenue. Much like the concept of operating profit margin (operating profit ÷ revenue), the OCF-to-revenue ratio tells you your cash flow return on revenue. This number should at least remain fairly constant over time; preferably it will increase.

Operating cash flow to total assets. The OCF-to-total assets ratio is significant because it helps you to evaluate whether you're producing cash flow as a result of an investment in balance-sheet assets, such as accounts receivable, WIP, or fixed assets. If this number is declining, it means that you have invested too much in fixed assets or that you've lost your focus on managing to a better bottom line and more efficient balance sheet.

Operating cash flow to equity. This ratio is a variation on the return-on-investment concept, using the most relevant measure of return—cash. Typically, one would not find a large amount of equity in a financial-advisory firm, but to the extent it exists it should, like any investment, be generating a positive and increasing cash flow return on equity.

For each of these ratios, healthy numbers for your advisory firm will depend on your business structure. It's helpful to compare your cash flow returns against industry benchmarks. But it's even more important to establish a baseline number for your practice and observe whether these cash flow returns are improving year to year.

Financial-Impact Analysis

Observing ratios in comparison with benchmarks and trends is interesting, but these numbers become even more revealing when you do a financial-impact analysis. The impact analysis translates the variance into a dollar amount. When you understand the magnitude of the problem, you're better able to focus on the solution. It may be tempting to downplay the problem when the ratio is off from the benchmark by only a fraction or a small percentage. In reality, a 1 percent variance can have a significant effect on the financial performance of your practice. One percent of a million dollars, for example, is real money.

To measure that financial impact, you must identify your target. This may be a benchmark derived from the *FPA Financial Performance Study,* or your firm's best year, or even an arbitrary number. The point is to compare your firm's number with the number to which you aspire. For example, let's say that your practice's revenue is $1,000,000 and your target operating profit margin is 25 percent (as determined by the industry benchmark), thus $1,000,000 × .25 = $250,000. Your financial statements indicate that your operating profit margin is only $100,000, or 10 percent of revenues. Based on the industry benchmark, that means you're $150,000 short of the amount appropriate for your firm.

So how do you use this information? Now that you've uncovered the magnitude of the problem, you can go back to your analysis and focus on the causes of low profitability—namely, a low gross profit margin, poor expense control, or insufficient revenue volume to support your overhead. What do you look at first?

Improving profitability requires following a logical, four-step process:

1. Cut costs.
2. Improve gross profit margin.
3. Increase volume.
4. Raise prices (if you have discretion to do so).

The most immediate way to attack low profitability is to determine which costs you can eliminate. This may mean making some hard choices, such as laying off staff, subletting space in your office, or imposing restrictions on purchases. Advisers often find these choices difficult to make because they assume that such cuts will seriously damage the business. But let's look at things in perspective: if you're not making enough to get the firm on the road to financial independence—plus provide a sufficient return to invest in your practice so that you can serve clients better—then you've already begun to damage your business. What steps are you going to take to make things right? Is it easier to cut costs or to increase revenues? Is it easier to adjust pricing or to be more selective about which clients you take on? Is it easier to train staff to be more effective or to lay them off? When it adds up to a $150,000 problem in a $1,000,000 practice, the steps required are probably a combination of all of these and more.

Obviously, the problem is even more acute in small practices because there are probably not as many areas to cut costs and still serve clients well. For many small practices, recognizing this dilemma becomes the catalyst for their decision to merge with another firm.

Productivity Analysis

For the purists in the financial-advisory business, "productivity" has a negative connotation because it conjures up images of the old brokerage environment. But regardless of how one views sales organizations, such as big brokerage and insurance companies, there is an indisputable economic logic to maintaining and increasing productivity. When an advisory firm does not maintain and build a reasonable level of productivity, its profitability will be undermined. With declining profitability, the firm has less to reinvest in the business, which it needs to do to maintain quality service for clients. Ultimately, productivity isn't just about money; it's about enhancing client service and the firm's reputation as a business.

Indeed, evaluating productivity is an essential part of a firm's financial management, and there are a number of ways to assess it:

- ◆ Revenue per client
- ◆ Gross profit per client
- ◆ Operating profit per client
- ◆ Revenue per total staff
- ◆ Revenue per professional staff
- ◆ Operating profit per total staff
- ◆ Operating profit per professional staff
- ◆ Clients per total staff
- ◆ Clients per professional staff

In isolation the ratios don't tell you much, but by evaluating the trend over a period of three or more years in each of these categories, you can observe what's happening to the business. For example, there is a point at which continuing to serve certain clients no longer makes economic sense. An adviser may decide—perhaps for altruistic reasons—to accept clients with assets below a minimum threshold, but that should be the exception, not the rule. To be effective in delivering services to the core client base, the core client relationships must be profitable and productive.

The productivity ratios should increase over time. A firm is likely to experience temporary aberrations in which the ratios decline, but by and large, owners should be able to rely on these ratios as indicators for when to add either professional or administrative staff. Such indicators are also useful in negotiating goals with staff and giving clarity to when staff should be added. As a general guideline, in an up market, it's prudent to add staff before you are at full capacity; in a flat or down market, it's best to wait until you're at or over capacity before adding staff. Of course, one of the other factors driving this decision will be how the additions to staff are paid—either variable amounts (commission) or fixed amounts (salary).

The Search for Solutions

H OW DO YOU translate the rules of financial management into practical applications for your business? Let's look at a few of the most common strategies advisers use to create business—referral agreements and joint ventures, practice acquisitions, and investments in new initiatives.

Referral Agreements and Joint Ventures

Financial advisers love joint ventures and referral agreements. They perceive them as low-cost, low-risk ways to expand their business. But by definition, joint ventures and referral agreements are designed to be short-lived: either they work extraordinarily well, and the larger advisory firm, CPA firm, or bank swallows the smaller advisory firm up whole, or they fail abysmally.

Joint ventures and referral agreements should not be confused with building one's referral network or developing informal alliances. In a referral agreement, whether it's a formal joint venture or not, two parties formally combine their strengths to shore up each other's weaknesses and systematically capture more business. A CPA firm, for example, may want a referral agreement with a financial-advisory firm so that it can deliver financial advice to its clients; or a financial adviser may seek a joint venture with a law firm to make legal advice and document preparation readily available to its clients. Usually one of the entities generates new business and the other provides expert services. Ideally the parties to the agreement would bring both strengths to the table, but that's rarely the case.

The referral-agreement model works best when both parties share in the risk and return, have an explicit commitment to each other to support the initiative, and have a clear vision of what they're trying to accomplish with the model. These arrangements fail when the relationship becomes one-sided, when success is measured simply in terms of short-term financial results, or when there is no clear strategic framework for why the agreement should work.

As with any new strategy, when considering a referral agreement, you must first clarify how this method of sale will build on the strengths of each firm, differentiate your firm from those competing for the same type of clients, be responsive to a specific market, and match your definition of success. For example, you may be an adviser specializing in very high-net-worth individuals with complex financial needs, especially in the tax management and estate-planning areas. To further extend your brand and deepen your relationship with clients, you might align with an accounting firm or a law firm that has that expertise and make those services part of your core offering to your clients. The challenge for you is to define what your firm is offering and distinguish it from what's offered by every other firm in your market, including accounting or law firms. Can you package these strengths in a way that makes their delivery more cost effective, or efficient, or integrated than what's currently available in the market? Is the proposition a compelling one for your target clients? Can you realistically project business through such an affiliation? And is the agreement the most effective way to allocate your resources?

Once you're clear about the type of client you're going to pursue and serve through the referral agreement, you'll need to define the functions each party will perform and determine who is accountable for each one. This requires being clear about the protocols for how clients will be handled throughout—from introduction, to intake, to document collection, to providing the service, to billing and collecting the fees. Who will be accountable for each step? What will the final product or service look like? How will you ensure quality control? How will you report back to the other parties on what is happening with specific clients? How will you resolve conflicts? How will you distribute the proceeds?

In joint ventures and referral agreements each side of the relationship should also have someone whose mission is to manage that relationship. Each party essentially becomes the other's client, and the relationship cannot be taken lightly. Some structured approach to communication must be in place, as well as a process for regularly examining what's working and what isn't. Be clear about the measurable objectives. How will you define success? Will it be the acquisition of new clients? Greater profitability? Greater share of wallet?

As you lay out the plan, it will become easier to develop a financial model that can help you evaluate whether a referral agreement is a logical business decision. For example, to increase assets and attract more clients, many advisers make the mistake of overpaying for referrals they receive from other professionals. That's why it's essential to understand the economics of your own business.

One adviser, for example, asked us to provide guidelines on the compensation structure for a joint venture he planned to set up with a CPA firm. The plan called for the CPA firm to refer its clients to the advisory firm through a joint venture, which would expand the adviser's offering and bring in incremental revenue. According to the accountant, the rule of thumb for the industry was a 25 percent payout on all revenues in perpetuity. Like all rules of thumb, this one took on a life of its own—whether or not it was logical or in the best interest of the firm providing the professional services.

We tried to help this adviser understand that a referral fee is part of direct expense, not part of overhead—in other words, a cost of goods sold. We believe that advisory firms should try to keep their direct expenses at around 40 percent, and they will need to pay for referrals or joint venture fees out of this amount. Direct sales and professional service outside of the joint venture or referral agreement are also direct expenses. So if, as in this example, an adviser pays 25 percent of total revenue from a client to the joint venture partner in perpetuity, that leaves only 15 percent to pay for the analysis, consulting, and implementation of the client's plan. This may be acceptable the first year, but it certainly is not acceptable in subsequent years because eventually the client bonds with the adviser and puts more demands on the firm. The "salesperson" provides only the introduction, not the ongoing services that give rise to all the future costs.

If the referral source requires some sort of trailing fee to provide legitimate leads, then the advisory firm needs to limit the payout to an amount it can afford. It's hard to justify more than a 10 percent ongoing trail (perhaps with 20–25 percent up front); in fact, 5 percent may be more appropriate and ideally for three to five years, not into perpetuity. If you pay a high referral fee in perpetuity, eventually you will have to ask if it's prudent to try to build your business around the low value clients these referrals become. Imagine the dilemma. Do you return the calls from the full-fee clients first or the calls from the clients for whom you've discounted your fees under the referral agreement? Do you provide the same degree of service to clients from the joint relationship? Which clients are you most concerned about losing? At some point, as your firm reaches capacity, you might, in fact, hope to lose some of those clients, because the "haircut" on them is so much larger than on clients you attracted through other means. Ultimately that outcome is not in the best interests of the client or the venture.

In many cases, for the same amount of effort, advisers could get high-value clients and not have to add overhead to support lower-margin business. The only exception to this is if they use the "unique sales method" strategy, in which most of their business comes from such a conduit. That way, they have a low-cost, efficient means of serving and supporting those clients. In other words, they build a service-delivery model around the economics of the relationship.

If your firm is using a joint venture or referral agreement to generate incremental business and that agreement is not integral to your firm's overall vision and strategy, the arrangement is probably not a good idea. Eventually you'll find that managing the relationship siphons off your time and you risk acquiring less-valuable business. Over time, that type of model will seriously erode your margins and your interests. Joint ventures and referral agreements can work, but only if the business purpose, the economics, and the commitment are right for your business.

Practice Acquisitions

To pump up volume quickly, many advisory firms acquire books of business from other advisers. Practice acquisitions are a great way to go, providing you don't overpay. Sellers will almost always rely on a rule of thumb—a multiple they read in the trade press or hear at a cocktail party. Your responsibility is to define the economics of the target practice—as we have shown in chapter 9—with charges to both fair compensation for the owner as well as all overhead expenses.

In financial terms, value is measured by projecting cash flow and discounting it at an appropriate risk rate (or required rate of return). To simplify this process, you can apply a capitalization rate to current free cash flow to come up with a value. For a buyer, this would be the most conservative way to measure value. Each year, we receive inquiries from advisers interested in unraveling deals they committed to several years before. Most of these dissatisfied owners have assumed a substantial book of clients who do not fit their target market but whom they now feel obligated to serve; others find there is insufficient cash flow from the practice to support the terms of the buyout and still have enough left over to pay themselves adequately for their time invested. Clearly, the "greater fool theory," which says that there will always be a buyer regardless of price, lives large in the advisory world. The causes are legion, but the biggest reason may be the lack of understanding of how businesses are valued and what the economic drivers for advisory firms are.

The problems we see with practice acquisitions typically fall into five categories:

1. **Not enough potential future income per client.** Many practices, especially those that depend on commissions, have already consumed the lion's share of the income in the form of front-end loads and insurance commissions. Even those that are fee-based may not have much life left in future income if the clients need to begin withdrawing principal. The question is not how much revenue the client base has generated in the past but rather how much it's likely to generate in the future.

2. **Clients who are too old.** Other practices are like depleted oil wells. There may be a little bit of the good stuff left at the bottom,

but the buyer will be investing in a practice that has a short life. If so, this can turn out to be a very expensive purchase, even on an earnout, because these formulas generally assume high growth in perpetuity.

3. **Price based on rules of thumb.** It's not uncommon for advisers selling practices to cite recent publications and articles in the trade press that encourage transactions by pumping up the price multiples. But a rule of thumb, by definition, relies on the past, not the future. In other words, the rule implies that the business will continue at least at the same level it has maintained in the past. If I were a seller, I would always rely on rules of thumb because these values will be the highest available. If I were a buyer, I would dismiss these rules for one simple reason: most small practices are sold on an earnout, and it's impossible to know what multiples of gross revenue a practice has sold for until the earnout period is over. To our knowledge, no studies have yet been published that revisit the price realized through the term of the earnout. The prices agreed to when the deals are consummated, which form the basis for the published rules of thumb, are rarely the prices the sellers actually realize through the earnout.

4. **Insufficient cash flow to support the purchase.** Sellers tend to focus on gross revenue rather than net income or cash flow in an acquisition. According to both the 2001 and 2003 *FPA Financial Performance Study,* the average operating costs of a practice hover around 45 percent of gross revenue. If you add to that the cost of administrative and professional labor—including the seller's, which you have to consider no matter what—the margins get very tight. So the question is, at the current rate of income, at what point can you expect to break even on the purchase?

5. **Lack of capacity.** One of the great surprises for many practitioners is the time it takes to transfer these client relationships. You can do it by adding staff, improving technology, or working ungodly hours. Or you can do it by accepting a certain level of attrition among clients who are not economically practical to serve. This brings up a moral question for the seller, however: Are you doing your low-end clients justice by selling them to somebody who does not want to take care of them?

So, is buying a practice a bad idea? Not necessarily. In spite of the risks, growth through acquisition still presents a viable opportunity for advisers to expand their practices quickly, but they must apply the same common sense to acquiring a practice as they do to counseling their clients. Investing in due diligence and critical analysis, including financial analysis, is essential before signing on the dotted line. Before buying a practice, every buyer should consider at least these six questions:

1. **How independent is the source of the deal, whether broker, investment banker, or other source?** Independence has been a professional battle cry for many advisers, but they often seem to value it less when engaging help for their businesses. Advisory firms commonly use intermediaries or business brokers—including online services—that represent both sides of a transaction. For the sake of expediency, advisers would rather have one person facilitate the deal; that way they can share the cost. That choice comes with a risk: the broker's goal is to see that the deal gets done, not to advocate for one side or the other. Obviously this can be good or bad, but you may never know. That's why it's prudent always to have an independent set of eyes—such as your attorney, your CPA, or an experienced merger-and-acquisition adviser—review the deal before you execute. What's more, many issues are complex and tricky and require a professional opinion from an expert on matters related to tax, liability, noncompetition agreements, and other terms in the deal.

2. **Can the practice reward me for both my labor and my risk?** In conventional valuation theory, analysts make adjustments for things like personal expenses, compensation, and the true cost of doing business before they apply a multiple or capitalization rate to the free cash flow of the enterprise. Because so many advisers do not differentiate between their compensation and their revenue minus expenses, this concept is often difficult for them to grasp. But one of the real costs of running an advisory practice is professional labor. In other words, if you were an employee of the business (which in fact you are), what would your labor be worth? In assessing the value of a practice, add dollars to reflect this cost and deduct it from the revenues along with all other expenses in the business to come up

with a bottom-line number. The bottom line will be the business's operating profit, or the return for your risk of buying and owning the business. That's the number that should be capitalized, not the gross. We have seen far too many practices that have a large gross but cannot afford to pay their owners fairly and produce a profit or a return on ownership.

3. **Is there a more effective way to deploy my resources?** You have a finite amount of time, money, and energy. Is buying an overvalued practice with limited growth potential the best deployment of those resources? For example, if the seller is asking $400,000, might you be better off investing those same dollars—or even a fraction of those dollars—into your own marketing, your own reputation, and your own efforts? This question is especially important to consider if you're not already part of the practice and therefore are uncertain whether the clients will continue with you. Could you achieve your net-return goal just as quickly, and for less money, without this acquisition?

4. **Is the acquisition a good cultural fit?** The excitement of consummating a deal often causes people to bypass the most basic question: Will this relationship work? Before you acquire a practice, be sure to understand the philosophy, the processes, and the reasons for the outgoing adviser's recommendations to his or her clients. If your approach—or your target clientele—conflicts with the seller's, the potential for attrition is very high. This may sound obvious, but we have seen far too many buyers who think they can change the way acquired clients buy products and services from their adviser. Ask yourself how you will do this. Trashing the approach used by the outgoing adviser is not usually a formula for success.

5. **Do I have the capacity to serve this client base?** You may be tempted to skim off the top clients and ignore the others—a choice that could make it easier to manage the capacity problem of taking on all of the new business. That's your call. But recognize that especially in the early years, you will need to expend an extraordinary effort to keep these clients in the fold, to make them feel valued, and to provide them with the kind of service that they've come to expect or that they truly desire. You should put together an operating plan for how you will serve these clients and with what frequency, then

determine if there are enough hours in the day for you to handle them in addition to your current client base.

6. **Have I evaluated all of the hidden risks?** Every acquisition has the potential for risks that are not apparent at the outset. These problems could involve compliance or client satisfaction, or they could take the form of past recommendations made by the firm that are now time bombs ready to explode. In the ideal world, you would have the opportunity to do a client satisfaction survey before you acquire the practice; several good and relatively inexpensive tools in the market are available for this. At a minimum, you will want to engage an independent compliance consultant to perform due diligence on the seller's practices and procedures before you commit. Both of these steps can be covered in your letter of intent, which is normally the prelude to the purchase agreement. Any reluctance on the seller's part to these kinds of evaluations raises a big red flag.

Investments in New Initiatives

Most advisers are awash in opportunity. A good idea comes down the pike about once a week—new markets, new services, new people, and so on. Some people in this business probably waste more money on new initiatives than they make on managing their business right.

The most common initiatives are special marketing efforts and hiring new people to open up a new market or to offer a new service. For either one, you need to define your expectations of return. Think of it in these terms: When you help manage your clients' performance expectations on their investments, you usually have to temper their enthusiasm with a conversation about the risk/return relationship. In your business, you must ask the same question: What is a reasonable return on my investment for these new initiatives, and when should the returns be realized? The amount of the return will vary, but you should attempt to calculate how much business you would need to do to generate both a return on the investment and a reasonable return for the risk you're taking.

Rules of thumb are always questionable, but it's generally a good idea in a service business to establish a time horizon of eighteen to twenty-four months within which you'll begin realizing a return. That horizon is relatively short, but the length is dictated by the nature of these investments, which are often geared to producing a return in a short time. So it's best to keep your expectations in line with that hope.

Afterword

ADVISERS SEEM TO fall into two groups, with two very different outlooks. The positivists say, "If things are so bad, why do I feel so good?" The fatalists are likely to ask, "If things are so good, why do I feel so bad?" The first group has no need to believe in Eden or the Apocalypse. They stand tall in the face of a storm. They're consistent with their clients, whether the markets are up or down. Their clients rely on them, and their practices continue to grow.

The fatalists don't see the opportunity that comes wrapped in adversity. They are ebullient in good times and deeply depressed in bad. They are victims. They don't know which way to turn, yet they're unwilling to make business decisions that will put them on the road to recovery. Eventually, the clients are the ones giving the advice and driving the decisions in these practices.

Positivists are more likely to recognize that fulfillment comes from having a vision and taking steps to achieve that vision. The reality for many advisers today is that they must make a quantum leap in how they structure and manage their practices if they're going to realize their goals.

Dale Turner, a retired minister in Seattle who for many years gave compelling sermons and now shares his wisdom through a weekly column in the *Seattle Times,* once wrote, "Although it is never good to pretend that problems do not exist, it is wise to look beyond the problems to the possibilities in each situation. When Goliath came against the Israelites, the soldiers all thought, 'He's so big; we can never kill him.' But David looked at the same giant and said, 'He's so big; I can't miss.' "

Many of us in the world of financial services tend not to truly look to the future. In fact, we often rely on the past as a predictor of our future. We make investment decisions based on a five- or ten-year history and refer to future events as no more than repetitions of past cycles, with no change possible or to be contemplated. We make hiring decisions based on our past experiences and on the candidate's résumé of past jobs. We assume that we can procure new clients exactly the same way we did when we were in our growth phase, and we think all future clients will respond to our advice the way our first clients did.

The tendency to rely on the past is understandable. It's comfortable. It's what we know. We can't see around corners or over hills, so we make decisions based on what is obviously and directly in front of us or right behind us. As Rev. Turner also wrote, "It's odd, isn't it, that as children we were afraid of the dark? Now, as adults, we are afraid of the light."

The quality of the light in the business of financial advice is different now. Success does not come as easily. Jack Welch, the accomplished former chairman of General Electric Co., applied the concept of "the quantum leap" to management, believing that business leaders have to take their heads out of the muck, out of the details, to look beyond their current travails. For advisers to be successful business owners and managers going forward, they'll have to acknowledge that assumptions have changed and therefore their approach to business will require that quantum leap.

In this book, our discussion of the financial-advisory business and the disciplines we recommend for working successfully within it are based on certain assumptions:

♦ The rate of organic growth in revenue will be slower.
♦ Time and margins will continue to be under pressure.
♦ It will be increasingly difficult to recruit, retain, and reward good people.
♦ Competition from new sources is increasing, and it will be more difficult for an adviser to differentiate his or her firm.
♦ Clients will be more demanding.

If you accept any of these assumptions as true, can you afford to content yourself with the status quo of practice management? Will you accept the consequence of that choice as fate, or will you embark on a strategy that allows you to take control of your destiny in light of these new challenges?

We've found that the most effective leaders of financial-advisory practices have in common certain approaches to doing business:

♦ They have a very clear idea of their strategy and positioning.
♦ They offer career paths for their staff and a compensation plan that reinforces their strategy.
♦ They have created leverage, improved capacity, and reduced their firm's dependency on them for growth.
♦ They have a systematic process for gathering client feedback.
♦ They consistently measure and monitor their firm's operating performance.
♦ They have an enlightened approach to managing for profits.

As a business owner, you need a strategy that will create momentum for your practice and differentiate it in the market it serves. It has become apparent in looking at the truly successful advisory firms that any strategy can work, as long as the owner is focused and makes a clear commitment to the pace and direction of growth. Strategy is not about marketing; it's about where a firm commits its resources. A strategy defines what you want your business to be and serves as a decision-making filter as you allocate your resources to implement your plan. Without that framework, it will be difficult for you to define your optimal client, the client-service experience, the organizational structure best suited to satisfy clients' needs, your pricing strategy, and your approach to compensation.

Armed with your strategy and the lessons in this book, you can go a long way toward creating the optimal practice model. But reaching that goal will require one more thing: your leadership. As Jim Collins says in his inspiring book *Good to Great: Why Some Companies Make the Leap ... and Others Don't* (HarperCollins, 2001), it's not enough to have every seat on the bus filled; you must make sure you have the right people on the bus. That begins with you.

Essential to embracing your role as a business leader is understanding that leadership and management are not the same thing. Leadership is the art of creating a vision and attracting followers to that vision. Management is the process of overseeing and implementing the details that will fulfill the vision. In his book *Principle-Centered Leadership* (Simon & Schuster, 1992), management guru Stephen Covey explains that "Leadership deals with direction—with making sure that the ladder is leaning against the right wall. Management deals with speed. To double one's speed in the wrong direction, however, is the very definition of foolishness. Leadership deals with vision—with keeping the mission in sight—and with effectiveness and results. Management deals with establishing structures and systems to get those results."

In every business, including small ones, you need both good management and good leadership. We discussed how to evaluate whether you need to hire a CEO, COO, or general manager to help you deal with the myriad of management issues you'll face. That is a staffing issue, requiring that you identify the business need, define the work and the desired outcomes, and prepare a profile of the ideal candidate for the role. To some extent, hiring a manager is an economic question, but it also compels you to first explore the role in the organization that you can effectively and passionately embrace.

However you manage the enterprise, the leadership of the business is ultimately up to you as its owner. For inspiration, we return to Collins's *Good to Great*. Perhaps better than most, Collins has identified the principles that can serve as your guideposts through the process of building a great financial-advisory business. His ten principles are indeed excellent tenets by which to run your business:

1. Build your business in a cumulative fashion.
2. Focus on who should be on the bus.
3. Remember that leadership is not a variable.
4. Have the discipline to confront the brutal facts.
5. Make decisions based on understanding, not bravado.
6. Have a culture of discipline to stick to your direction.
7. Use technology accelerators that can take your business to a different level.
8. Reduce the firm's dependency on you.
9. Build a business that leaves something enduring, not just one to make money.
10. Build your company on core values that do not change.

Throughout this book, we've attempted to weave these principles into the methodology for practice management. But remember, the business is not your dream; it is the vehicle to help you achieve your dreams. We hope this book has set you on a course to build an enterprise that's responsive to your dreams.

Appendix

THROUGHOUT THE BOOK, we have referred to helpful worksheets in the appendix. We hope you will find these templates useful in getting organized and focused on building and growing a dynamic practice.

Practice-Management Assessment

TAKE THIS QUIZ and find out how your firm stacks up.

HUMAN CAPITAL

1. My key staffers envision their position within my firm in three years' time as

    a) significantly promoted

    b) more efficient at the same responsibilities

    c) about the same as now

    d) nonexistent

2. Raises and variable compensation at my firm are

    a) determined by an objective formula related to firm strategy, position levels, and responsibilities

    b) determined by an objective formula unrelated to firm strategy, position levels, and responsibilities

    c) subjective but somewhat consistent from year to year

    d) subjective and inconsistent from year to year

3. Job descriptions at my firm

    a) clearly outline responsibilities and play a key role in performance evaluations

    b) clearly outline responsibilities

    c) are somewhat outdated and/or vague

    d) are nonexistent

4. The culture at my firm

    a) is stated clearly in a written statement and plays a key role in performance evaluations

    b) is discussed informally and is intuitively or implicitly understood by staff

    c) hasn't really been discussed

    d) is detracting from optimal firm performance

LEADERSHIP

5. When it comes to what the firm will look like in five years, I

    a) have a clear vision and a good idea of what it will take to get there, and so do my staff

    b) have a clear vision but I'm not really sure how to make it happen or how to include staff in the process

    c) am not really sure what it will look like, but I wish I had time to think about it

    d) don't particularly care

6. My "lieutenants" or go-to people at the firm

    a) have responded well to my coaching and make my life much easier than when I was going solo

    b) were thrown in at the deep end but have stepped up to the challenge

    c) were thrown in at the deep end and are struggling to keep up

    d) don't exist; it's just me

7. If my staffers need to talk with me,

    a) they are comfortable walking through the door and talking with me

    b) they have been told they can stop by anytime, but they don't

    c) they need to schedule an appointment in advance

    d) they should talk with somebody else

8. When I discover counterproductive or inappropriate behavior by my staff,

    a) I follow fair and objective standard procedures to enforce changes in their behavior

    b) I schedule an appointment with them to talk it over

    c) I bring it up outside of work in a social situation

    d) There is no way of discovering such behavior

STRATEGIC PLANNING

9. If someone were to talk with any of my employees, would they be able to identify why the firm is in business?

    a) Yes—everyone from the management team to the administrative staff can answer this.

b) The management team knows, but others do not.

c) Some employees know; others don't.

d) I don't know, and no one else can really articulate it either.

10. Tomorrow, you unexpectedly have to leave your business. If you returned in five years, would your business as you know it still exist?

a) Absolutely—we have crafted a well-thought-out strategic plan.

b) Very likely—we have a strong management bench committed to the overall direction of the firm.

c) Not sure—there are currently many different types of products and services we offer to all kinds of clients, so it would be hard to say.

d) No—I drive the firm and its strategy, and make decisions independently. If I went away, this firm would survive for a while but be gone in five years.

11. Your recruiting department comes to you with a sheaf of résumés. How do you decide whom to hire?

a) I review our current needs, but also review the strategic plan to decide if this person will move us incrementally toward our goals.

b) I make sure we have enough revenue to support an additional person—so I evaluate his/her book of business.

c) I make sure the person has the résumé and references appropriate for the position.

d) I don't handle hiring decisions. That's why we have a human resources department.

12. When a significant competitor begins aggressively penetrating your market, how confident are you that your firm is positioned to preserve market share?

a) 95% confident—our business plan is built to concentrate our resources and our focus on a product/service offering our clients prefer.

b) 75% confident—I think we're in pretty good shape. Our business plan discusses marketing and other measures to deal with competition.

c) 50% confident—it'll be a challenge, but we've known our clients long enough that they'll stay with us.

d) <20%—not that confident, but I suppose we'll make some changes to fee charges, etc., to keep clients at our firm.

CALCULATE YOUR SCORE

Give yourself two points for every A, one point for every B, no points for a C, and subtract one point for each D.

21 or higher

On track: Based on your responses to these questions, it appears that you have laid some solid groundwork for building your firm up and out. Now that the basics are in place, there is time to tackle more sophisticated and complex issues. Will the compensation program and career paths at your firm continue to inspire, motivate, and retain staff? If not, how should you change them? Do any of your staff exhibit characteristics that make them attractive as partner candidates? If so, when should the transition to partner begin, and how will it take place? Does the vision for your firm still meet your personal definition of success for your own life? How can you bring the two into alignment?

11 to 20

Back to basics: It looks like you have some momentum in your business, but now would be a good time to update and standardize your business practices to prevent roadblocks to success. Do your people know what they're supposed to be doing and how they're being evaluated? Do they know what they can do to advance their careers and improve their compensation? Do you know? It's difficult to retain good staff without communicating a clear picture of what their future could look like within your firm if they excel. And it might be difficult for you to maintain your interest if you're not compelled by where the firm is headed in the intermediate term. Have you strategized lately about where your firm is headed or checked to make sure it's still on course?

5 to 10

Prioritize: There are likely more than a few things at your firm that could be going more smoothly, but trying to tackle them all at once will likely be more overwhelming than productive. Identify the root causes of your firm's pains and prioritize them. Are there any minor issues whose resolution will placate the troops? Put those at the top of the list. Next, is your strategy clear to you and your staff? Does it make sense? Nailing this difficult issue down will help stabilize the firm and allow other pieces to start falling into place. Other human-capital or leadership-training issues can be placed further down on the to-do list, but they shouldn't be ignored or forgotten.

Less than 5

Take stock: If you've been in the business for only a few short years, take heart. Managing a business is very different from being a practitioner, and there's no substitute for experience. However, training can definitely help. Are you finding it difficult to manage people? Or to plan for the future of your business? Budget for resources to address the areas where you need help. A modest investment in leadership coaching or strategic planning now can help you avoid costly missteps in the future.

If you've been in the business for a while, are you sure the direction your firm is headed is still a good fit for you? If you want your business to grow, you'll need to be able to inspire, motivate, and monitor your staff, which will be impossible if you're not excited about the direction of the business or interested in the people working for you.

Analysis of Top Twenty Clients

LIST YOUR TOP TWENTY CLIENTS, based on the alignment of their needs with your strengths and the size, profitability, and enjoyment level of the relationship.

What consistent themes emerge from the top twenty list? Either an individual aspect of the client profile or some combination may point to a

CLIENT NAME	FINANCIALS		CHARACTERISTICS			
	Annual billings ($000)	Estimated profit before tax (%)	Estimated net worth ($000)	Assets with firm ($000)	Annual income ($000)	Age
Example: John Doe	40	10	5,000	2,500	300	57
1.						
2.						
3.						
4.						
5.						
6.						
7.						
8.						
9.						
10.						
11.						
12.						
13.						
14.						
15.						
16.						
17.						
18.						
19.						
20.						

segment of the population that could be a focus group. Examples of those segments include:

♦ Chiropractors
♦ Clients in their mid-fifties to mid-sixties dealing with transition to retirement
♦ Net worth of $5M or more, requiring investment-consulting services

Profession	Other	Other	Other	Service 1	Service 2	Service 3	Service 4	Service 5	Service 6	Service 7	Service 8
					SERVICES						
Chiropractor				X	X		X				

IN THE TABLE BELOW, estimate the impact of acquiring twenty more clients within each of the segments identified from the consistent themes in the top twenty list.

SEGMENT	Annual firm revenue impact ($000)	Firm overhead expenses impact ($000)	Firm profitability before tax impact (%)
Example: Chiropractors	800	10000.00	4.50

Firm AUM impact ($M)	Staffing impact: Professionals (no. of staff)	Staffing impact: Technical support (no. of staff)	Staffing impact: Administrative (no. of staff)	Other
100	1	1	0	

Self-Evaluation

THE FOLLOWING performance evaluation illustrates how one company's value system (PILLAR) is linked to its performance-evaluation criteria. Be sure that your evaluation questions are linked to your own company's business strategy and unique value system.

Name: _____   Date: _____

Position: _____   Office: _____

The purpose of self-evaluation is to:

Passion for Excellence
Integrity
Lifetime Learning
Leading by Example
A Balanced Life
Respect for Others

THE PILLAR

♦ Assess your strengths and the areas you feel need development
♦ List accomplishments for evaluating advancement opportunities
♦ Generate ideas for discussion with your performance coach

PASSION FOR EXCELLENCE

Please list your strengths:

_____

Please list the areas you would like to improve (identify at least two):

_____

Please list your accomplishments during the evaluation period:

_____

INTEGRITY

Please comment on your commitment to the professional and ethical standards of the profession:

Please comment on your willingness to address unethical or inappropriate behavior on the part of clients and colleagues:

LIFETIME LEARNING

Please comment on the adequacy of the training (internal and external) you have received in terms of developing your skills:

Please comment on other training you have sought or attained outside of the training provided by our firm:

What additional or new responsibilities have you assumed since your last evaluation?

What areas do you believe you should be emphasizing to further your career-development goals?

LEADING BY EXAMPLE

Describe how you have acted as a role model or mentor to others in the office or firm:

What would you suggest as a means of enhancing the firm's spirit within our office?

A BALANCED LIFE

The amount of overtime you worked was:

More than expected/desired ❏
As expected/desired   ❏
Less than expected/desired   ❏

Comments:

Please comment on the balance between your professional and personal life:

RESPECT FOR OTHERS

Please comment on your working relationships with your colleagues and the firm's clients:

What other questions or areas would you like to address during your evaluation session?

Performance Evaluation
for Professional Staff

THE FOLLOWING performance evaluation illustrates how one company's value system (PILLAR) is linked to its performance-evaluation criteria. Be sure that your evaluation questions are linked to your own company's business strategy and unique value system.

Evaluation of: _____ Evaluation period: _____

Position: _____ Evaluator's name: _____

Instructions: The purpose of performance evaluation is to acknowledge areas of strong performance, provide reinforcement, and discuss areas for development.

Evaluators are encouraged to:

♦ Reinforce areas of strength by commending good performance

♦ Identify areas needing development and provide specific examples

♦ Establish a measurable goal for primary areas of performance where improvement or additional experience is needed

Passion for Excellence
Integrity
Lifetime Learning
Leading by Example
A Balanced Life
Respect for Others

THE PILLAR

RATINGS: A rating of "good" should be given if a person is meeting the expectations and job requirements for his or her level of experience and is progressing at a normal rate of advancement.

Excellent	Exceptional performance; consistently exceeds expectations
Very good	Frequently exceeds expectations
Good	Meets expectations and fulfills all responsibilities

Source: © Moss Adams LLP

RATINGS: *(continued)*

Needs improvement   Requires development; does not consistently meet
                         expectations

Unacceptable   Performance is below the acceptable level

Not rated   Not enough basis for evaluation or not applicable

PASSION FOR EXCELLENCE

Demonstrates enthusiasm and pride in the work she/he performs.

❑ Excellent   ❑ Very good   ❑ Good
❑ Needs improvement   ❑ Unacceptable   ❑ Not rated

Comments: _____

Completes projects accurately and within budget.

❑ Excellent   ❑ Very good   ❑ Good
❑ Needs improvement   ❑ Unacceptable   ❑ Not rated

Comments: _____

Solves technical problems effectively. Demonstrates objectivity and an
analytical ability. Demonstrates a solid base of technical knowledge.

❑ Excellent   ❑ Very good   ❑ Good
❑ Needs improvement   ❑ Unacceptable   ❑ Not rated

Comments: _____

Speaks and writes clearly and effectively.

❑ Excellent   ❑ Very good   ❑ Good
❑ Needs improvement   ❑ Unacceptable   ❑ Not rated

Comments: _____

Demonstrates good listening skills.

❑ Excellent   ❑ Very good   ❑ Good
❑ Needs improvement   ❑ Unacceptable   ❑ Not rated

Comments: _____

Meets client-service expectations. Provides ideas, recommendations, and solutions to clients that improve results.

❏ Excellent ❏ Very good ❏ Good
❏ Needs improvement ❏ Unacceptable ❏ Not rated

Comments: _____

INTEGRITY

Demonstrates an interest in personal growth and expansion of his/her knowledge base.

❏ Excellent ❏ Very good ❏ Good
❏ Needs improvement ❏ Unacceptable ❏ Not rated

Comments: _____

Displays objectivity, identifies important issues, asks relevant questions, reaches sound conclusions, and considers the potential impact before recommending actions.

❏ Excellent ❏ Very good ❏ Good
❏ Needs improvement ❏ Unacceptable ❏ Not rated

Comments: _____

Demonstrates an understanding of our clients' needs.

❏ Excellent ❏ Very good ❏ Good
❏ Needs improvement ❏ Unacceptable ❏ Not rated

Comments: _____

LIFETIME LEARNING

Continues to develop his/her talents, skills, and knowledge.

❏ Excellent ❏ Very good ❏ Good
❏ Needs improvement ❏ Unacceptable ❏ Not rated

Comments: _____

Uses technology tools and resources effectively to perform assignments.

❑ Excellent ❑ Very good ❑ Good
❑ Needs improvement ❑ Unacceptable ❑ Not rated

Comments: _____

LEADING BY EXAMPLE

Demonstrates a positive attitude toward company goals and contributes to maintaining high morale in the office.

❑ Excellent ❑ Very good ❑ Good
❑ Needs improvement ❑ Unacceptable ❑ Not rated

Comments: _____

Takes responsibility for actions and accepts responsibility for mistakes.

❑ Excellent ❑ Very good ❑ Good
❑ Needs improvement ❑ Unacceptable ❑ Not rated

Comments: _____

Acts as a role model or mentor for others.

❑ Excellent ❑ Very good ❑ Good
❑ Needs improvement ❑ Unacceptable ❑ Not rated

Comments: _____

A BALANCED LIFE

Provides a positive example to others as a person who is able to balance professional responsibilities while also maintaining balance in his/her personal life.

❑ Excellent ❑ Very good ❑ Good
❑ Needs improvement ❑ Unacceptable ❑ Not rated

Comments: _____

RESPECT FOR OTHERS

Treats colleagues with respect and consideration.

❏ Excellent   ❏ Very good   ❏ Good
❏ Needs improvement   ❏ Unacceptable   ❏ Not rated

Comments: _____

Keeps managers informed of progress and job status.

❏ Excellent   ❏ Very good   ❏ Good
❏ Needs improvement   ❏ Unacceptable   ❏ Not rated

Comments: _____

Responds to suggestions and input from others in a respectful manner.

❏ Excellent   ❏ Very good   ❏ Good
❏ Needs improvement   ❏ Unacceptable   ❏ Not rated

Comments: _____

PERSONNEL MANAGEMENT

Demonstrates a commitment to the development of other people in the office.

❏ Excellent   ❏ Very good   ❏ Good
❏ Needs improvement   ❏ Unacceptable   ❏ Not rated

Comments: _____

Conducts performance reviews that are comprehensive, productive, and timely.

❏ Excellent   ❏ Very good   ❏ Good
❏ Needs improvement   ❏ Unacceptable   ❏ Not rated

Comments: _____

Recognizes staff members for good performance and coaches them when improvement is needed.

❏ Excellent   ❏ Very good   ❏ Good
❏ Needs improvement   ❏ Unacceptable   ❏ Not rated

Comments: _____

ENGAGEMENT MANAGEMENT

Plans and manages engagements to achieve efficiency and develop the skill of staff members.

❏ Excellent   ❏ Very good   ❏ Good
❏ Needs improvement   ❏ Unacceptable   ❏ Not rated

Comments: _____

MARKETING AND PRACTICE DEVELOPMENT

Is actively involved in professional and community activities.

❏ Excellent   ❏ Very good   ❏ Good
❏ Needs improvement   ❏ Unacceptable   ❏ Not rated

Comments: _____

Initiates actions that create new client opportunities.

❏ Excellent   ❏ Very good   ❏ Good
❏ Needs improvement   ❏ Unacceptable   ❏ Not rated

Comments: _____

ADDITIONAL COMMENTS _____

OVERALL PERFORMANCE SUMMARY

In general, this individual is:

❏ Exceeding performance expectations and progressing rapidly
❏ Meeting performance expectations and progressing very well
❏ Meeting most performance expectations and progressing satisfactorily
❏ Meeting some performance expectations; needs improvement
❏ Currently not meeting performance expectations

PRIMARY STRENGTHS

What primary strengths were identified during the evaluation?

1. _____

2. _____

3. _____

AREAS FOR DEVELOPMENT

Identify key areas where improvement or additional experience is needed.

1. _____

2. _____

3. _____

Develop a goal for each key area for development.

1. _____

2. _____

3. _____

Staff member's comments _____

SIGNATURES

I acknowledge that I have had an opportunity to discuss this evaluation with my performance coach.

_____   _____

Staff Member   Date

Evaluated by:

_____   _____

Performance Coach   Date

Reviewed by:

_____   _____

Partner   Date

Source: © Moss Adams LLP

Upstream Evaluation

THE FOLLOWING performance evaluation illustrates how one company's value system (PILLAR) is linked to its performance-evaluation criteria. Be sure that your evaluation questions are linked to your own company's business strategy and unique value system.

Evaluation of: _____   Evaluation period: _____

Your position: ❏ Client service
                 ❏ Administrative staff

Instructions: The purpose of performance evaluation is to acknowledge areas of strong performance, provide reinforcement, and discuss areas for development.

Evaluators are encouraged to:

♦ Reinforce areas of strength by commending good performance

♦ Identify areas needing development and provide specific examples

♦ Establish a measurable goal for primary areas of performance where improvement or additional experience is needed

Passion for Excellence
Integrity
Lifetime Learning
Leading by Example
A Balanced Life
Respect for Others

THE PILLAR

During my work with this individual, I have found that he or she (*please comment in each area*):

PASSION FOR EXCELLENCE

Is technically proficient, provides good advice, and is able to answer my technical questions.

❏ Consistently ❏ Usually ❏ Sometimes ❏ Rarely ❏ Not rated

Evaluator's comments: _____

Demonstrates a passion for excellence in his or her work.

❏ Consistently ❏ Usually ❏ Sometimes ❏ Rarely ❏ Not rated

Evaluator's comments: _____

Provides noticeably superior service to our clients.

❏ Consistently ❏ Usually ❏ Sometimes ❏ Rarely ❏ Not rated

Evaluator's comments: _____

INTEGRITY

Recognizes the full range of our clients' needs and recommends value-added services that improve their business results.

❏ Often ❏ Occasionally ❏ Seldom ❏ Never ❏ Not rated

Evaluator's comments: _____

Delegates challenging work that is appropriate for my level of experience.

❏ Delegates work appropriately
❏ Delegates assignments that are too easy
❏ Delegates assignments that are too difficult
❏ Not rated

Evaluator's comments: _____

Includes me in meetings with clients.

❏ Often ❏ Occasionally ❏ Seldom ❏ Never ❏ Not rated

Evaluator's comments: _____

Source: © Moss Adams LLP

LIFETIME LEARNING

Helps me to develop my skills by providing opportunities for growth and challenge.

❏ Often   ❏ Occasionally   ❏ Seldom   ❏ Never   ❏ Not rated

Evaluator's comments: _____

LEADING BY EXAMPLE

Conducts productive and timely performance evaluation meetings. *(Please check "Not rated" if this person is not responsible for giving you written evaluations.)*

❏ Consistently   ❏ Usually   ❏ Sometimes   ❏ Rarely   ❏ Not rated

Evaluator's comments: _____

Makes time to be accessible when I have suggestions, questions, or problems.

❏ Consistently   ❏ Usually   ❏ Sometimes   ❏ Rarely   ❏ Not rated

Evaluator's comments: _____

Listens attentively and is interested in my opinions and thoughts.

❏ Listens intently   ❏ Is usually attentive
❏ Often does not hear what I am saying   ❏ Not rated

Evaluator's comments: _____

Gives me recognition for my contributions and efforts.

❏ Often   ❏ Occasionally   ❏ Seldom   ❏ Never   ❏ Not rated

Evaluator's comments: _____

A BALANCED LIFE

Understands that it is important for staff members to maintain balance in our lives.

❑ Consistently   ❑ Usually   ❑ Sometimes   ❑ Rarely   ❑ Not rated

Evaluator's comments: _____

RESPECT FOR OTHERS

Treats people with respect.

❑ Consistently   ❑ Usually   ❑ Sometimes   ❑ Rarely   ❑ Not rated

Evaluator's comments: _____

What do you most like about working with this individual?

_____

Do you have any suggestions for improving your working relationship?

_____

How to Use Compensation Benchmarking and Salary-Survey Data

THE FOLLOWING TABLE is an excerpt from the 2003 *FPA Compensation and Staffing Study*. It illustrates how to interpret and use the data tables the study provides for each job title. Whatever analysis or salary survey you employ to review your business should consider the same questions outlined here, so that you can be sure you're using the data appropriately and effectively.

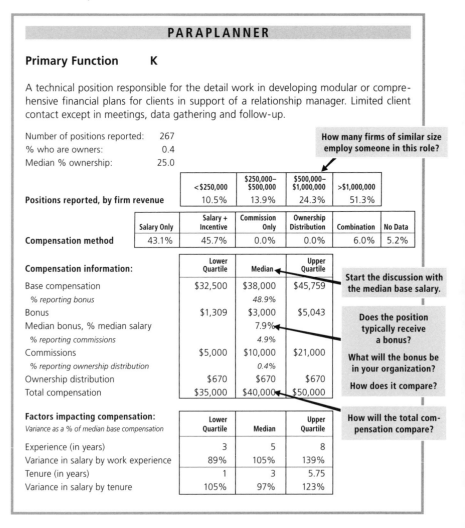

PARAPLANNER

Primary Function   K

A technical position responsible for the detail work in developing modular or comprehensive financial plans for clients in support of a relationship manager. Limited client contact except in meetings, data gathering and follow-up.

Number of positions reported: 267
% who are owners: 0.4
Median % ownership: 25.0

How many firms of similar size employ someone in this role?

	<$250,000	$250,000–$500,000	$500,000–$1,000,000	>$1,000,000
Positions reported, by firm revenue	10.5%	13.9%	24.3%	51.3%

	Salary Only	Salary + Incentive	Commission Only	Ownership Distribution	Combination	No Data
Compensation method	43.1%	45.7%	0.0%	0.0%	6.0%	5.2%

Compensation information:	Lower Quartile	Median	Upper Quartile
Base compensation	$32,500	$38,000	$45,759
% reporting bonus		48.9%	
Bonus	$1,309	$3,000	$5,043
Median bonus, % median salary		7.9%	
% reporting commissions		4.9%	
Commissions	$5,000	$10,000	$21,000
% reporting ownership distribution		0.4%	
Ownership distribution	$670	$670	$670
Total compensation	$35,000	$40,000	$50,000

Start the discussion with the median base salary.

Does the position typically receive a bonus?

What will the bonus be in your organization? How does it compare?

How will the total compensation compare?

Factors impacting compensation: Variance as a % of median base compensation	Lower Quartile	Median	Upper Quartile
Experience (in years)	3	5	8
Variance in salary by work experience	89%	105%	139%
Tenure (in years)	1	3	5.75
Variance in salary by tenure	105%	97%	123%

What impact does the location of your firm, the employee's level of experience, and his/her secondary functions typically have on base pay for this position?

PARAPLANNER (continued)

	CFP
CFP certificate holder	14.6%
Variance in salary if CFP certificant	111%

	<$250,000	$250,000–$1,000,000	$1,000,000+	No Data
Population of local market				
% of positions reported by population	18.4%	23.3%	54.3%	4.0%
Variance in salary by population	83%	95%	105%	

	No Secondary	0	N, Q	Other
Most common secondary functions				
% reporting secondary function	49.8%	13.1%	6.4%	30.7%
Variance in salary by secondary function				
As a % of median base compensation	100%	101%	89%	
As a % of total compensation	100%	106%	94%	

	Full-Time	Part-Time	No Data
Full- vs. part-time:			
% of positions reported	83.5%	15.7%	0.7%

	Lower Quartile	Median	Upper Quartile
Annual salary for part-time	$19,500	$25,000	$30,000

Based on the simple analysis described above, establish a range of base compensation for the employee and then determine the final compensation inside the range based on the characteristics of that individual.

Balance Sheet

RECORD YOUR DOLLAR BALANCES in the dollars column ($). Remember that total assets need to equal total liabilities and equity. Divide all dollar balances by total assets to arrive at the percentages (%).

	Dollars and Common Size Percentages	
	($)	(%)
1 Cash	_____	_____
2 Marketable securities	_____	_____
3 Accounts receivable—net	_____	_____
4 All other current assets	_____	_____
5 Total current assets (sum 1 to 4)	_____	_____
6 Property	_____	_____
7 Furniture, fixtures, and equipment	_____	_____
8 Other fixed assets	_____	_____
9 Total gross fixed assets (sum 6 to 8)	_____	_____
10 Less accumulated depreciation	_____	_____
11 Total net fixed assets (9 minus 10)	_____	_____
12 Other long-term assets	_____	_____
13 Total assets (sum 5, 11, and 12)	_____	_____

	Dollars and Common Size Percentages	
	($)	(%)

LIABILITIES AND EQUITY

14 Notes payable _____ _____

15 Taxes payable _____ _____

16 Accounts payable _____ _____

17 Accruals _____ _____

18 Current portion of long-term debt _____ _____

19 All other current liabilities _____ _____

20 Total current liabilities
(sum 14 to 19) _____ _____

21 Long-term debt _____ _____

22 Other noncurrent liabilities _____ _____

23 Total long-term liabilities
(sum 21 and 22) _____ _____

24 Total liabilities
(sum 20 and 23) _____ _____

25 Equity (net worth) _____ _____

26 Total liabilities and equity
(sum 24 and 25) _____ _____

Source: © Moss Adams LLP

Income Statement

RECORD YOUR DOLLAR EXPENSES in the dollars column ($). Divide all dollar expenses by the total revenue to arrive at the percentages (%).

	Dollar and Common Size Percentages	
	($)	(%)
1 Asset-management fees		
2 Planning and consulting fees		
3 Securities commissions—current		
4 Securities trails		
5 Insurance commissions —new or first year		
6 Insurance renewals		
7 Other revenue		
8 **Total revenue** (sum 1 to 8)		**100%**
9 Nonowner professional salaries		
10 Commissions paid and other direct expenses		
11 Owners' draws or base compensation		
12 **Total direct expense** (sum 9, 10, 11)		
13 **Gross profit** (8 minus 12)		
14 Advertising, public relations, and marketing		
15 Auto expenses		
16 Charitable contributions		

	Dollar and Common Size Percentages ($)	(%)
17 Client appreciation	_____	_____
18 Depreciation and amortization	_____	_____
19 Dues (clubs)	_____	_____
20 Dues (professional)	_____	_____
21 Employee benefits	_____	_____
22 Equipment leases and purchases	_____	_____
23 Insurance	_____	_____
24 Office expense	_____	_____
25 Other salaries	_____	_____
26 Payroll taxes	_____	_____
27 Professional services	_____	_____
28 Rent	_____	_____
29 Repairs and maintenance	_____	_____
30 Software and hardware expense	_____	_____
31 Tax and licenses	_____	_____
32 Training and continuing education	_____	_____
33 Travel and entertainment	_____	_____
34 Utilities, phone, fax, and online service	_____	_____
35 All other expenses	_____	_____
36 Total overhead (sum 14 to 35)	_____	_____
37 Operating profit (13 minus 36)	_____	_____

Source: © Moss Adams LLP

Calculations for Ratios

PROFITABILITY RATIOS

♦ *Gross profit margin*

(Gross profit ÷ total revenue) × 100% = gross profit margin

(_____ ÷ _____) × 100% = _____

♦ *Operating profit margin*

(Operating profit ÷ total revenue) × 100% = operating profit margin

(_____ ÷ _____) × 100% = _____

♦ *Overhead percentage*

(Total overhead ÷ total revenue) × 100% = overhead percentage

(_____ ÷ _____) × 100% = _____

♦ *Average total income per owner*

(Owner's base draw + operating profit) ÷ no. of owners = average total income per owner

(_____ + _____) ÷ _____ = _____

PRODUCTIVITY RATIOS

♦ *Revenue per professional*

Total revenue ÷ no. of professionals = revenue per professional

_____ ÷ _____ = _____

♦ *Revenue per staff*

Total revenue ÷ no. of total staff = revenue per staff

_____ ÷ _____ = _____

♦ *Clients per professional*

Total clients ÷ no. of professionals = clients per professional

_____ ÷ _____ = _____

♦ *Clients per staff*

Total clients ÷ no. of total staff = clients per staff

_____ ÷ _____ = _____

♦ *Operating profit per professional*

Operating profit ÷ no. of professionals = operating profit per professional

_____ ÷ _____ = _____

♦ *Operating profit per staff*

Operating profit ÷ no. of total staff = operating profit per staff

_____ ÷ _____ = _____

CLIENT-SELECTION RATIOS

♦ *Revenue per client*

Total revenue ÷ no. of clients = revenue per client

_____ ÷ _____ = _____

♦ *Assets under management per client*

Assets under management ÷ no. of clients = assets under management per client

_____ ÷ _____ = _____

♦ *Gross profit per client*

Gross profit ÷ no. of clients = gross profit per client

_____ ÷ _____ = _____

♦ *Operating profit per client*

Operating profit ÷ no. of clients = operating profit per client

_____ ÷ _____ = _____

Cash Flow Calculator

ACCOUNT ITEM

1 Net income after tax _____

2 Depreciation and amortization _____

3 +/– Changes in accounts receivable _____

4 +/– Changes in inventory _____

5 +/– Changes in other current assets _____

6 +/– Changes in accounts payable _____

7 +/– Changes in accrued expenses _____

8 +/– Changes in income tax payable and deferred taxes _____

9 +/– Changes in other current liabilities _____

10 +/– Changes in other noncurrent liabilities _____

11 Operating cash flow (OCF)

12 +/– Changes in marketable securities _____

13 +/– Changes in long-term investment _____

14 +/– Changes in gross fixed assets _____

15 Nonrecurring gain (loss) _____

16 +/– Changes in intangible and other noncurrent assets _____

17 Investing cash flow (ICF)

18 *Cash flow before financing* (sum 11 and 17) _____

19 +/– Changes in short-term bank debt _____

20 +/– Changes in long-term bank debt _____

21 +/– Changes in subordinated debt _____

22 +/– Changes in capital stock _____

23 –Dividends paid _____

24 +/– Adjustments to retained earnings _____

25 +/– Changes in minority interest _____

26 Financing cash flow (FCF)

27 Total cash flow (sum 11, 17, and 26) _____

Index

accounting
accrual, 146
cash-basis, 145–146
fundamentals of, 137–138
Accredited Investors, 25–26, 39–40
accrual accounting, 146
administrative staff, use of, 54–56
Advisor Impact, 5, 39, 40, 56
Client Audit process, 43, 45, 46
advisory firms, top challenges facing, 6–7
affiliation model, 66–70
American Express Financial Advisors, 68
American Marketing Association, 46
Applied Business Solutions, 16
assets
current, 140
fixed, 140–141
Atlas Shrugged (Rand), 95

Bachrach, Bill, xiv, 23
balance sheets
analysis of, 162–168
description of, 139–143, 214–215
Balasa, Mark, 15–16
BAM Advisor Services LLC, 68
base pay, 117–118, 120–124
benchmarking
compensation, 121–124, 212–213
hiring employees and, 86–88

Beyond Survival: A Guide for Business Owners and Their Families (Danco), 7
bonuses and incentives, 118–119, 124–128
Boston Private, 24
Bowen, John, xiv
break-even analysis, 159
Bruckenstein, Joel, xv, 4, 54

capabilities (core) perspective, 23
cash-basis accounting, 145–146
cash flow calculator, 220
cash flow statements
analysis of, 168–169
description of, 146–148
CEO, hiring a, 104
common mistakes, 105–109
CFA Institute, 151, 152
Christopher Street Financial, Inc., 17–18, 45
client
analysis of, 26–27, 194–197
demands, 2–3
entrepreneurs and relationships with, 56–58
satisfaction affected by growth, 60
selection ratio, 219
surveys, 39–47
Client Audit process, 43, 45, 46
Collins, Jim, 185, 186
common sizing, 160

About the Authors

Mark C. Tibergien is a principal at the accounting firm Moss Adams LLP in Seattle. He is partner in charge of the Business Consulting Group for the firm, chairman of the Securities and Insurance Niche, chairman of the Business Valuation Niche, and a past member of the firm's executive committee. He has been working with public and private companies on matters related to business management, succession planning, and strategy formulation since 1973.

Mr. Tibergien has a particular expertise in consulting on management issues within the financial-services industry, having consulted with hundreds of broker-dealers, financial advisers, investment managers, insurance companies, and other financial-services organizations in the United States, Australia, and Canada. He served as president of the Western Washington chapter of the International Association for Financial Planning (IAFP) (now the Financial Planning Association), chairman of the Northwest Regional Council of IAFP, and an elected member of the IAFP National Executive Committee.

As a nationally known adviser, speaker, and workshop leader within the securities and insurance industries, Mr. Tibergien delivers between fifty and sixty presentations to industry conferences each year on topics related to strategy, industry trends, practice management, and mergers and acquisitions. In 1996, the Washington Society of CPAs recognized him as the "outstanding instructor of the year." Every year since 1999, *Accounting Today* has recognized him among the "100 Most Influential" in the accounting profession. In 2003, *Financial Planning* magazine and Financial Planning.com named him as a "Mover & Shaker" in their annual review of industry professionals, and in 2002 and 2003, *Investment Advisor* magazine rated him among the "25 Most Influential" in the financial-services industry.

Mr. Tibergien was president of Management Advisory Services before it merged with Moss Adams in January 1994. He was a vice president of Willamette Management Associates, an investment-management and business-valuation firm headquartered in Portland, Oregon, and a writer for *Investment Dealers' Digest* in Chicago. He received his education from Bay de Noc College and the University of Wisconsin, Stevens Point.

Readers may contact the author at mark.tibergien@mossadams.com.

Rebecca Pomering is a principal at the accounting firm Moss Adams LLP in Seattle and specializes in management consulting to the financial-advisory industry. Since joining Moss Adams in 1997, Ms. Pomering has provided consulting services to financial-advisory firms, broker-dealers, and independent trust companies on issues of business management, compensation, and organizational design. She is a certified Senior Professional of Human Resources and the head of Moss Adams's compensation consulting practice as well as a key member of the Moss Adams Securities & Insurance Niche consulting team. Her work in this industry focuses on strategic planning and consulting on issues related to compensation, practice management, organizational effectiveness, and succession planning.

Ms. Pomering manages more than a dozen annual industry research and benchmark projects on compensation and operating performance, including the Financial Performance and Compensation studies for the Financial Planning Association, the Broker-Dealer Financial Performance and Compensation studies for the Financial Services Institute, and the Million Dollar Round Table "Top of Table" operating performance study. She has been engaged as a speaker on financial-services-industry topics for such organizations as Schwab Institutional, Fidelity Investments, Raymond James Financial Services, Macquarie Bank, SEI Investments, American Express, ING Network, Alliance Bernstein, Columbia Funds, Financial Services Institute, and the Financial Planning Association and has coauthored articles published in the *Journal of Financial Planning* and other industry publications.

Ms. Pomering is an elected member of the Financial Planning Association's national board of directors. Before joining Moss Adams, she was the assistant controller at Thomas Kemper Soda Co. and an investment assistant with Franklin Financial Planning. She received a BS in finance and accounting from the University of Illinois, graduating magna cum laude.

Readers may contact the author at rebecca.pomering@mossadams .com.

About Bloomberg

Bloomberg L.P., founded in 1981, is a global information services, news, and media company. Headquartered in New York, the company has sales and news operations worldwide.

Bloomberg, serving customers on six continents, holds a unique position within the financial services industry by providing an unparalleled range of features in a single package known as the BLOOMBERG PROFESSIONAL® service. By addressing the demand for investment performance and efficiency through an exceptional combination of information, analytic, electronic trading, and Straight Through Processing tools, Bloomberg has built a world-wide customer base of corporations, issuers, financial intermediaries, and institutional investors.

BLOOMBERG NEWS®, founded in 1990, provides stories and columns on business, general news, politics, and sports to leading newspapers and magazines throughout the world. BLOOMBERG TELEVISION®, a 24-hour business and financial news network, is produced and distributed globally in seven different languages. BLOOMBERG RADIO℠ is an international radio network anchored by flagship station BLOOMBERG® 1130 (WBBR-AM) in New York.

In addition to the BLOOMBERG PRESS® line of books, Bloomberg publishes *BLOOMBERG MARKETS*® and *BLOOMBERG WEALTH MANAGER*® magazines. To learn more about Bloomberg, call a sales representative at:

London:	+44-20-7330-7500
New York:	+1-212-318-2000
Tokyo:	+81-3-3201-8900

FOR IN-DEPTH MARKET INFORMATION and news, visit the Bloomberg website at **www.bloomberg.com**, which draws from the news and power of the BLOOMBERG PROFESSIONAL® service and Bloomberg's host of media products to provide high-quality news and information in multiple languages on stocks, bonds, currencies, and commodities.